A SEASONAL
SOUTH LOUISIANA COOKBOOK

LOUISIANA
LEGACY
TODAY

THIBODAUX SERVICE LEAGUE

In loving memory of Ann Hebert Howell, a
founding member and the charter president of
Thibodaux Service League.

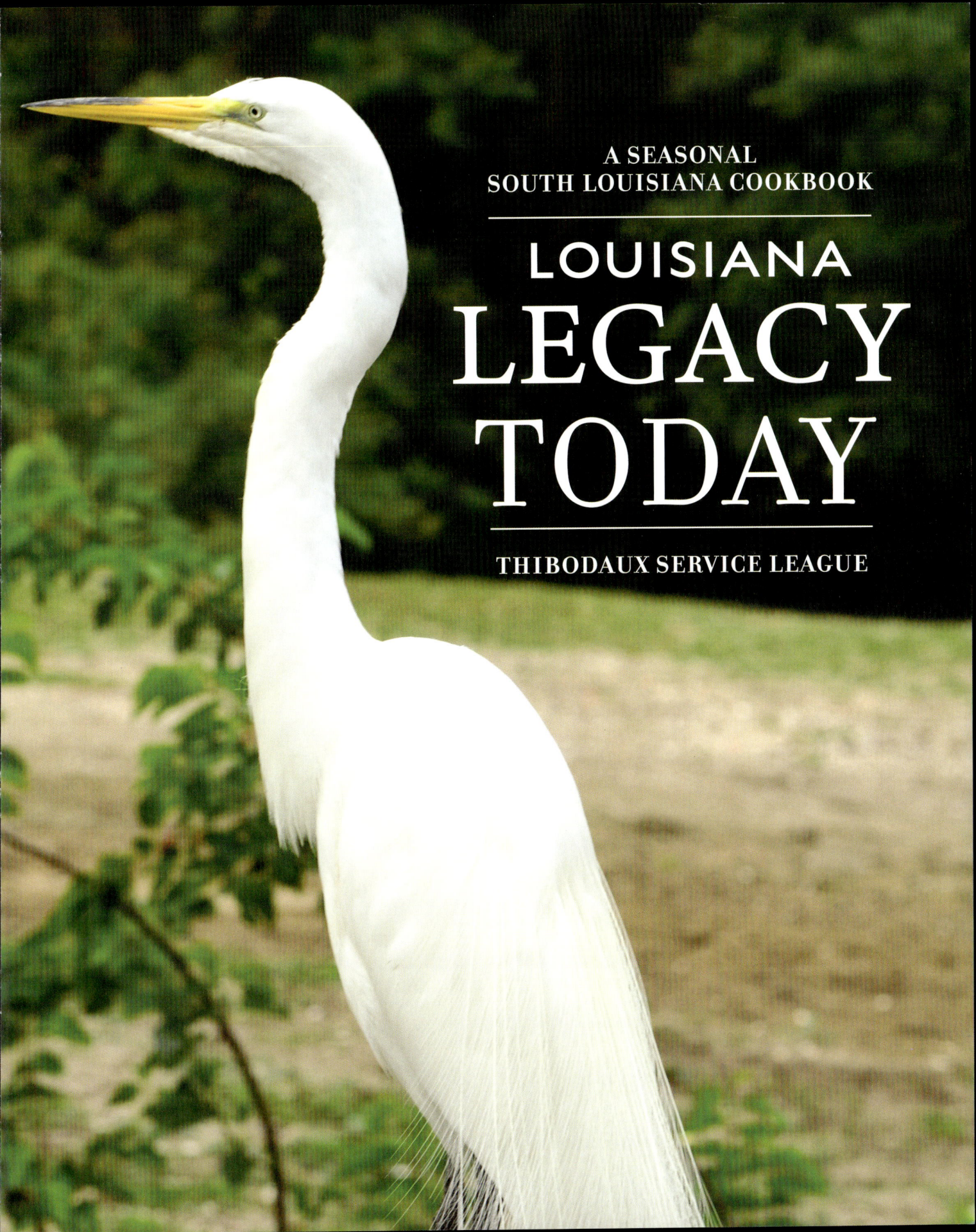

A SEASONAL
SOUTH LOUISIANA COOKBOOK

LOUISIANA
LEGACY
TODAY

THIBODAUX SERVICE LEAGUE

LOUISIANA LEGACY TODAY COOKBOOK COMMITTEE

Katherine Toups Elias   Anne Morgan Rodrigue

Jeanne Glaser Higgins   Stephanie Chiasson Toups

Courtney Fields Lichenstein

FOOD PHOTOGRAPHERS

Byron Landry   Craig Perque

COOKBOOK DESIGN

Amber Knight   Erica Verberne   Monica Stock

Akaira Sutton   Trisha Rabalais   Chelsi Navarre

Kayli Mato   Tessa Gautreaux

LANDSCAPE PHOTOGRAPHY

Ethan Blanchard Photography, LLC, page 152

Dinah Bynam, page 230

Noel Camardelle, page 188

Byron Landry, pages 100, 228

Kelly Landry, page 318

Photographs on pages 7, 12, 18, 120, 202, 267, 280,
350, 361 © 2019 Mandy Lens Photography

Photographs on pages 34, 64, 122, 332, 422, 432
© 2019 Tim Mueller Photography

Craig Perque, front cover, pages 16, 108, 238

Gibbs Robichaux, back cover, pages 8, 290, 330

ACKNOWLEDGEMENTS

Thibodaux Service League is grateful to all who helped in any way in the production of this cookbook. Recipe submitters have been noted with each recipe. Recipes have been tested, edited for conciseness, readability, procedure, oven temperatures and pan sizes. Ingredients are listed in the order needed. Exact can and package sizes are specified and substitutions noted when appropriate.

RECIPE GATHERING AND TESTING
Active and Provisional
Thibodaux Service League Members
from 2015- 2019

HOMES
Kelly Moreau Guin
Courtney Fields Lichenstein
Anne Morgan Rodrigue
Ashley Griffith Simoneaux
Stephanie Chiasson Toups

THIBODAUX SERVICE LEAGUE ADVISORY BOARDS
2015-2016 Board of Directors, Kristi Blakeman Gravois, President
2016-2017 Board of Directors, Ashley Perque Becnel, President
2017-2018 Board of Directors, Jamie Hebert Gros, President
2018-2019 Board of Directors, Katherine Toups Elias, President
2019-2020 Board of Directors, Keli Bonvillain Dantin, President

TABLE OF CONTENTS

FORWARD

by Marcel Bienvenu

I have over 500 cookbooks shelved in my home office. The collection began over 50 years ago when Aunt Git Broussard gave me a copy of the Betty Crocker New Picture Cook Book published in 1961. Not only did it contain over 1,850 recipes, but also offered "coordinated plans for delightful dinners, lunches and breakfasts," and "also instructions on how to freeze foods and suggestions for table settings."

A goodly amount of my collection are cookbooks to which I refer as "community cookbooks." Written and published by church groups, civic organizations, family compilation and even some by energy power companies. These have been my references and inspiration for over 30 years.

They all tell a story and many of them are like time capsules. I can usually tell the period in history in which they were published. For example, books from the 1800's and into the early 1900's, used measures like "a knob of butter, a wineglass of chicken broth, a loaf of sugar and a cupful of milk." Books from the mid-1950's have recipes that use cream of mushroom (sometimes referred to as American's béchamel) in casseroles or comfort foods. Some books that are now being published include not only "how to make a roux" but suggest that you can buy ready-made roux at your local Louisiana supermarkets. In our busy, busy lives, there's nothing wrong with taking short cuts when time is of the essence. I have no problem with purchasing containers of chopped "trinity" when I have an impromptu gathering.

Considering the many recipes that exist for gumbo, one of our south Louisiana iconic dishes, I look to my copy of The Louisiana Gumbo Cookbook (Acadian House Publishers) if I need a gumbo inspiration.

When I was approached to write the forward for the Thibodaux Service League's cookbook, I realized that I had the first edition and had used it a couple of times for research. When I worked and lived at Oak Alley,

I was surprised to learn that in this area, everyone eats fried fish with white beans and rice. What was all that about? In my hometown, we pair fried fish with potato salad.

While inspecting the recipes to be included in the new book, I noticed a recipe for pastalaya, which didn't appear in the older book. This dish is a relative newcomer to the cuisine of south Louisiana, and I recall my introduction to it in the 1980's when I worked at Oak Alley. It's very popular in the Terrebonne/Lafourche area, but I rarely see it in the Lafayette region. You'll find it in the new edition.

If you are crazy about the crawfish pies that are featured at the Firemen's Fair - yep, the recipe is in the new book. And speaking of our popular freshwater crustacean - crawfish - we've come a long way from only using these delectable mini-versions of lobsters for a boil, etouffee or pie. In this book, you'll find recipes for crawfish grilled cheese, crawfish deviled eggs and crawfish nachos.

I applaud the ladies of the Thibodaux Service League for compiling the recipes for this book that encompasses our broad Louisiana foodways, which includes German, French and Italian inspired dishes. Many of the recipes have been handed down from generation to generation. The kitchens in south Louisiana have always been the most important part of our homes and many times have been and continue to be the incubator for creating new dishes from what is at hand.

Color photographs showcasing our lush sub-tropical landscape, our popular festivals and of course, our distinctive cuisine are included in this new revision.

I know that this is a book to be treasured and my hope is that you will pass it on to friends and family, and visitors that venture to our south Louisiana paradise.

ABOUT

In 1982, the Thibodaux Service League published the Louisiana Legacy cookbook, a locally beloved collection of nearly 500 southern Louisiana recipes. The cookbook sold over 30,000 copies in the 1980's and continues to be sold today. This cookbook is not an attempt to redo the original Louisiana Legacy cookbook but to instead continue and expound upon it. The last sentence of Louisiana Legacy reads: "It is the children who hold the future: in them is the good of the past, the reality of the present and a hope for the best of both in the years to come. They, in the end, are our finest legacy." It is our sincere hope that this cookbook represents the "best of both"—that is, a combination of the lessons of the past and the enthusiasm and creativity of today in the southern Louisiana culinary world. With all this in mind, after years in the making, we present Louisiana Legacy Today by Thibodaux Service League. Wherever you may be, we hope this cookbook brings you a piece of Southern Louisiana—great food best shared with family and friends!

In the south, we are known for adding a pinch of this and a dash of that and for substituting certain ingredients to reflect our own personal style of cooking. This cookbook presents a collection of recipes based on each individual submitter's style of cooking. We encourage you to add your own flare where you see fit. Cooking is a story and you should tell it the way you like it.

"MAKING DO"

Life in South Louisiana has long been romanticized for its dramatic beginnings, its picturesque wildlife, its warm-hearted, happy, people, excellent food and historic folklore that can be found nowhere else in our country. These qualities hold true especially along Bayou Lafourche; here, where history has woven its spell for two centuries around a people strong in their independence and resourceful in their way of living. "Making do" with what nature has made available in these warm waters and fertile lands, they have shared an endless amount of bounty and creativity, shaping a lifestyle easy-going in its pace and rich in hospitality. With the abundance of fish, game, herbs and vegetables offered by an almost year-round growing season, "making do" comes naturally. Like gently cajoling, caressing mothers, cooks transform native foods into sumptuous delicacies; by adding to the basic ingredients bouquets des herbes, a dash of spices, a splash of brandy or rum, those who "stir the pot" ad lib genius. Inventive, robust and splendid, these culinary triumphs are a way of life; they are learned from childhood just as surely as breathing and eating, and just as naturally as the crawfishing, crabbing, hunting or numerous other occupations contributing to them, which come with growing up in this tranquil world. They are, really, a heritage; a gift shared through the years by one generation with the next.

Louisiana Legacy, 1982

SPRING

Spring usually arrives in Thibodaux in March, although sometimes it greets us as early as February or as late as April. The landscape completely changes, from the browns and grays of winter to bright greens and beautiful pinks, purples and yellows. Azaleas in Thibodaux are stunning and a welcomed change to residents. Carnival, crawfish and strawberry seasons kick off spring followed by Lent and the celebration of new life at Easter. Cinco de Mayo and the Fireman's Fair end the season on a festive note.

IN SEASON

ARTICHOKES	CORN	SQUASH
ARUGULA	GREEN BEANS	STRAWBERRIES
ASPARAGUS	MANGOES	THISTLE
BLACKBERRIES	RASPBERRIES	VIDALIA ONIONS
BLUEBERRIES	ROMAINE	WATERCRESS
BUTTER LETTUCE	SHALLOTS	ZUCCHINI

SPRING FAVORITES

The warm weather of spring is a welcomed change to
Thibodaux residents. Outdoor activities fill the calendar.
Fresh local crawfish, seafood, strawberries, blueberries,
artichokes and corn fill our happy bellies.

GRILLED ARTICHOKE WITH LEMON BUTTER

Serves: 4 to 6

2 to 3 whole artichokes

2 tablespoons extra virgin olive oil

1 tablespoon salt

½ teaspoon black pepper

½ teaspoon cayenne pepper

1 teaspoon garlic powder

1 to 2 clove(s) garlic, minced

¼ teaspoon lemon zest

¼ cup fresh parsley, chopped

fresh Parmesan cheese, grated

juice of 1 to 2 lemon(s)

½ cup butter

salt, to taste

capers, drained and rinsed (optional)

Jeanne Glaser Higgins

1. Trim ½ to 1 inch from stem end of artichoke.
2. Trim ½ inch off the top of artichoke.
3. Slice in half and steam until slightly tender, approximately 5 minutes. To steam, fill stock pot with approximately 1 inch of water, add artichokes and cover with top then bring to a boil.
4. Drain artichokes and let cool.
5. Remove the choke by scooping out with a spoon and trim prickly leaves.
6. On a baking sheet, drizzle artichokes with olive oil on both sides.
7. In a bowl, mix together salt, black pepper, cayenne pepper, garlic powder, minced garlic, lemon zest and parsley.
8. Spread seasoning mixture on top of and in between artichoke leaves.
9. Cut edge facing up, sprinkle with Parmesan cheese and a few squeezes of lemon juice.
10. Place on medium high grill, cut edge down to get a light char, approximately 3 to 5 minutes.
11. Flip artichoke and cook another 3 to 5 minutes until leaves can be pulled off easily.
12. Melt butter and mix with remaining lemon juice and salt to taste.
13. If using, add capers to butter mixture.
14. Serve artichokes with lemon butter for dipping.

CHEF DOMINIQUE M SCHEXNAYDER

HOMETOWN:
Houma, Louisiana

EDUCATION AND EXPERIENCE:
Chef Dominique earned a Bachelor of Science Degree in Culinary Arts with a concentration in Food and Beverage from Johnson and Wales University in Charlotte, North Carolina. Chef Dominique then worked at Restaurant August in New Orleans, was the Assistant Wine Director and Manager of Blue Restaurant and Bar in Charlotte, North Carolina, Chef at Dominique's Bistro and is now the owner and Executive Chef of Dominique's Wine Boutique and Bistro.

"My favorite thing about Thibodaux is the people. Genuine hospitality is something we take for granted. There is nowhere else in the world with people like we have here!"

STRAWBERRY SPINACH SALAD

Serves: 4

A perfect way to enjoy fresh Louisiana strawberries.

HONEY BALSAMIC STRAWBERRY VINAIGRETTE

1 cup fresh strawberries, tops removed

1 clove garlic

¼ teaspoon salt

¼ teaspoon pepper

¼ cup balsamic vinegar

¼ cup honey

¼ cup extra virgin olive oil

1 tablespoon Dijon mustard

SALAD

4 cups baby spinach

½ cup red onions, sliced

1 cup fresh strawberries, sliced

½ cup goat cheese crumbles

½ cup pecans

1. To make the vinaigrette, place all ingredients in a blender and puree until smooth.

2. Prepare the salad by combining spinach, red onions, strawberries, goat cheese, pecans and top with vinaigrette.

Chef Dominique Schexnayder

SEAFOOD SALAD WITH SPICY GARLIC VINAIGRETTE

Serves: 4

Make this HEALTHe Cafe favorite at home.

SALAD

8 ounces raw shrimp (125 to 150 count)

1 pound Louisiana crawfish tails

2 to 3 drops crab boil (optional)

pinch of salt

½ teaspoon garlic powder

¼ teaspoon cayenne pepper

½ teaspoon onion powder

juice from 1 lemon

salt and pepper, to taste

1 head of green leaf lettuce, chopped and washed thoroughly

2 Roma tomatoes, diced

1 avocado, thinly sliced

4 eggs, boiled and cut in half

½ cup shredded 4 cheese blend

8 ounces crab claw meat

SPICY GARLIC VINAIGRETTE

2 cloves garlic, finely minced

1/3 cup canola oil

3 tablespoons rice wine vinegar

juice from 1 lemon

2 teaspoons honey

¼ teaspoon cayenne pepper

pinch of salt

pinch of pepper

1. Bring medium size pot of water to boil.

2. Add the shrimp and crawfish to the pot.

3. Add a couple drops of crab boil, if desired, and a pinch a salt.

4. Once cooked and shrimp are pink, drain and transfer to a mixing bowl.

5. Add garlic powder, cayenne pepper, onion powder, lemon juice, salt and pepper to taste.

6. Divide all remaining ingredients amongst 4 large salad plates top with crabmeat and seafood mixture.

7. For dressing, combine garlic, oil, rice wine vinegar, lemon juice, honey, cayenne pepper, salt and pepper.

8. Mix thoroughly and pour evenly over each salad.

Claire Kopfler

LITE CRAB BISQUE

Serves: 8 to 10

Great lite version of the classic crab bisque that is both gluten and dairy free.

48 ounces low sodium chicken broth

2 cups Cajun vegetable trinity

3 cloves garlic, minced

1 pound frozen carrots

1 pound frozen corn

½ (13.66 ounce) can lite coconut milk

1 (13.66 ounce) can regular coconut milk

juice from 1 lemon

1 pound jumbo lump crabmeat

3 stalks green onions, chopped

salt and pepper, to taste

1. Bring 16 ounces of chicken broth to a boil in a large pot.

2. Add Cajun vegetable trinity and garlic.

3. Return to boil and continue cooking for approximately 5 minutes, stirring frequently until onions are softened.

4. Add remaining broth and carrots.

5. Bring to a boil then reduce to a simmer, continue cooking for 8 to 10 minutes.

6. Reduce heat to low, then using an immersion blender or food processor, blend ingredients until smooth.

7. Add corn, coconut milk, lemon juice, crabmeat, green onions, salt and pepper and simmer for a few minutes until flavors combine.

Claire Kopfler

CHICKEN AND
CRAWFISH TURNOVERS

Serves: 8 turnovers

If freezing, will keep longer if wrapped individually in plastic wrap.

1 bunch green onions, chopped

2 tablespoons butter

2 tablespoons flour

½ cup evaporated milk

¼ cup white wine

1 cup chicken broth and/or crawfish juice

1 teaspoon salt

1 teaspoon cayenne pepper

¼ teaspoon garlic powder

¼ teaspoon Tabasco sauce

3 ounces mozzarella cheese, grated

6 ounces mild Cheddar cheese, grated

1 (2 to 3 pound) deboned or rotisserie chicken, cubed

1 pound crawfish tails

3 (10 ounce) boxes Pepperidge Farm puff pastry shells (2 boxes for fuller turnovers)

1. Preheat oven to 400 degrees.
2. To make filling, sauté green onions and butter.
3. Add flour, blending thoroughly.
4. Slowly add milk, wine, broth and/or crawfish juice, salt, cayenne pepper, garlic powder and Tabasco sauce.
5. Cook until thick, stirring constantly.
6. Stir grated cheese into hot mixture and allow to melt.
7. Add cubed chicken and crawfish tails.
8. Cook on low approximately 5 minutes, then remove from heat and allow to cool.
9. To assemble turnovers, defrost pastry shells. Roll thin, keeping round shape.
10. Fill each with ½ cup filling. Fold over and seal by wetting the edges and pressing with a fork. Vent tops with fork.
11. Bake in oven for 8 minutes or freeze for later baking.
12. When baking frozen turnovers, bake for 15 to 20 minutes.

Amigas Club

SHRIMP AND ARTICHOKE CASSEROLE

Serves: 6 to 8

1 (14 ounce) can artichoke hearts, drained

4 tablespoons butter, divided

1 ½ pounds shrimp, peeled and deveined

1 clove garlic, chopped

1 onion or 4 green onions, chopped

¼ pound mushrooms, sliced or 4 ounce can, drained

1 (10 ounce) can cream of mushroom soup

½ cup mayonnaise

1 teaspoon Worcestershire sauce

1 tablespoon dry sherry

½ cup Parmesan cheese, grated

salt and pepper, to taste

1 (10 ounce) package frozen chopped spinach, slightly boiled and well drained

paprika, to garnish

breadcrumbs, to garnish (optional)

1. Preheat oven to 375 degrees.

2. In a medium saucepan, sauté artichokes in 2 tablespoons butter, drain and set aside.

3. In the same saucepan, in remaining butter, sauté shrimp until pink and cooked thoroughly.

4. Place sautéed artichokes and shrimp in a buttered 2 quart casserole dish or individual smaller ramekins.

5. In separate pan, sauté garlic, onions and mushrooms in 2 tablespoons butter.

6. After sautéed, add undiluted soup, mayonnaise, Worcestershire sauce, sherry, Parmesan cheese, salt, pepper and spinach.

7. Pour mixture over shrimp and artichokes.

8. Sprinkle dish with more Parmesan cheese and paprika.

9. May sprinkle breadcrumbs on top.

10. Bake in oven until bubbly, approximately 30 minutes.

Amigas Club

CRAWFISH NACHOS

Serves: 8

Also great with shrimp.

1 pound crawfish tails, cooked and coarsely chopped

1 ½ cups Cheddar cheese, grated

1 (2.25 ounce) can black olives, sliced

1 cup green onions, chopped

1 (4 ounce) can green chilies, chopped

½ cup mayonnaise

2 jalapenos, finely chopped

¼ cup onion, finely chopped

salt and pepper, to taste

nacho chips

1. Preheat oven to 350 degrees.
2. Combine all ingredients except nacho chips and mix well.
3. Mixture can be made ahead and refrigerated for a couple of days.
4. Just before placing into oven, spoon mixture onto nacho chips.
5. Bake for 5 to 7 minutes.
6. Serve immediately.

Paul Cummins

AUNT NELLIE'S
CORN MAUX CHOUX

Serves: 6 to 8

1 small onion, chopped

½ cup butter

1 (29 ounce) can whole corn, drained

2 (11 ounce) cans shoe peg corn or white corn, drained

1 (14.75 ounce) can cream style corn

1 (10 ounce) can Rotel

salt, to taste

1. Preheat oven to 350 degrees.
2. Sauté onion in butter.
3. Combine sautéed onions with remaining ingredients in a 9 x 13 inch pan.
4. Bake uncovered for 45 to 60 minutes or until liquid is dissolved.
5. Season with salt to taste.

Melanie Delaune

BLUEBERRY CRUNCH

Serves: 10 to 12

This dish tastes even better the next day!

PECAN CRUST

1 cup butter, softened

½ cup light brown sugar

1 ½ cups flour

½ cup pecans, chopped in food processor

CREAM CHEESE LAYER

2 (8 ounce) packages cream cheese

1 ½ cups sugar

BLUEBERRY FILLING

2/3 cup sugar

3 tablespoons cornstarch

dash of salt

1 cup water

1 pint blueberries

1 (12 ounce) container Cool Whip

Sally Webre

1. Do NOT preheat oven.
2. To make the pecan crust, mix butter and brown sugar until creamy.
3. Add flour and stir, then mix in pecans.
4. Spread mixture into a 9 x 13 inch buttered dish. Press into pan.
5. Place in cold oven, set at 350 degrees for 8 to 10 minutes. Watch carefully so it does not burn.
6. Remove from oven and allow to cool completely.
7. For cream cheese layer, mix cream cheese and 1 ½ cups sugar with a mixer until soft.
8. Spread on top of the pecan layer.
9. To make the blueberry filling, in a medium saucepan, mix together 2/3 cup sugar, cornstarch, salt, water and blueberries.
10. Bring to a boil and quickly lower the temperature to low, stirring often.
11. Cook mixture until it forms a creamy filling, approximately 10 minutes.
12. Remove from heat and allow to cool.
13. Spread the blueberry filling on top of cream cheese layer and then top with Cool Whip.
14. Refrigerate for a minimum of 1 hour prior to serving.

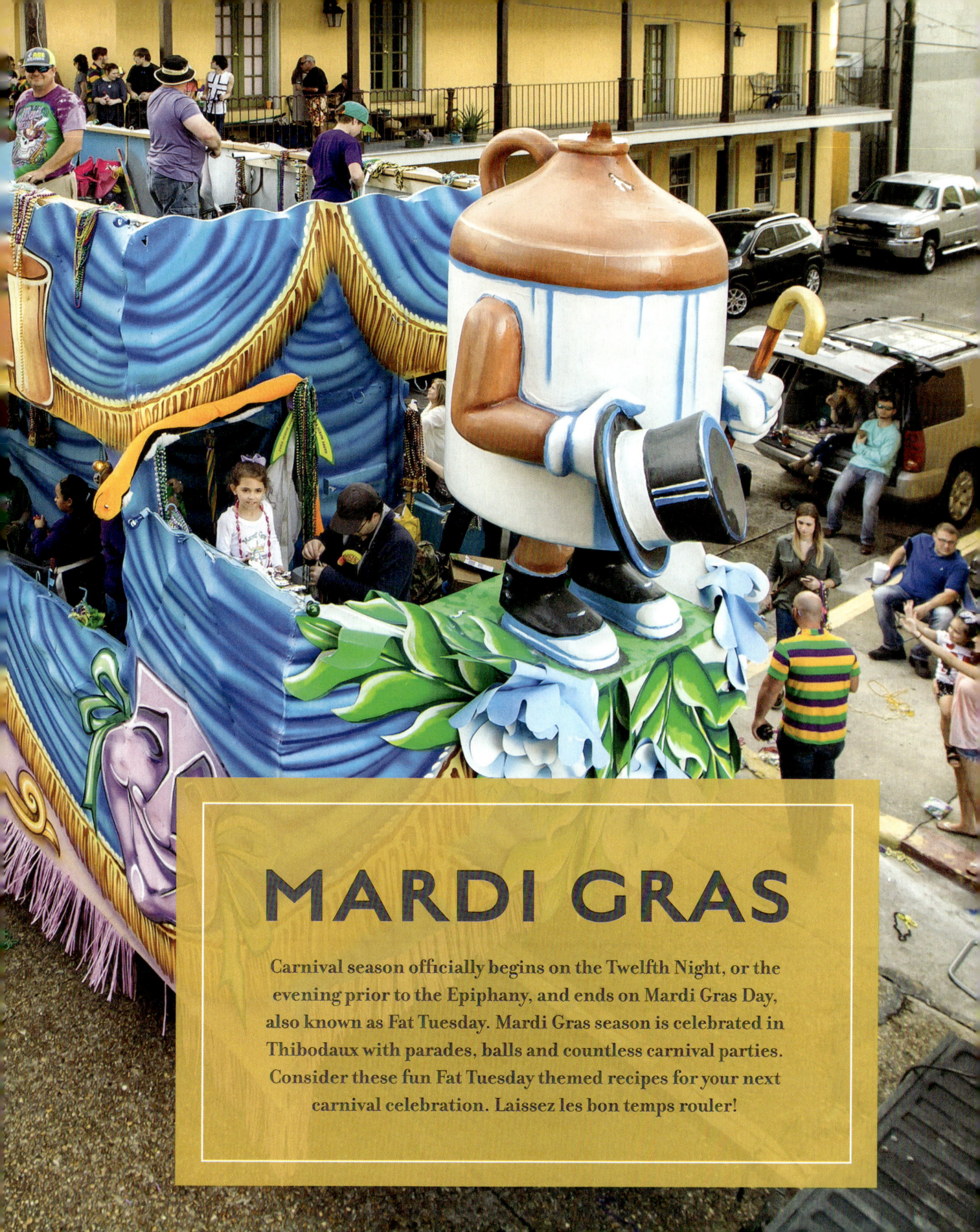

MARDI GRAS

Carnival season officially begins on the Twelfth Night, or the evening prior to the Epiphany, and ends on Mardi Gras Day, also known as Fat Tuesday. Mardi Gras season is celebrated in Thibodaux with parades, balls and countless carnival parties. Consider these fun Fat Tuesday themed recipes for your next carnival celebration. Laissez les bon temps rouler!

BOUDIN KING CAKE

Serves: 10 to 12

Form the bread into 2 loaves instead of a circle and serve it year round as Boudin-Cracklin Bread.

1 pound frozen bread dough, thawed (recommend L&N Grocery Store brand)

2 links (approximately ¾ pound) boudin, removed from casing

4 to 8 ounces pepper jack cheese, thinly sliced (optional)

2 tablespoons butter, melted

CANE SYRUP AND CRACKLIN TOPPING

1/3 cup cane syrup

1/3 cup cracklin crumbs

½ cup green onions, sliced

PEPPER JELLY AND BACON BITS TOPPING

1/3 cup pepper jelly

1/3 cup bacon bits

Anna Falcon Arthurs

1. Preheat oven to 350 degrees.
2. Roll out the thawed bread dough until it is long and narrow.
3. Place the loose boudin filling on the flattened bread dough, leaving 2 inches from the sides.
4. If using the pepper jack cheese option, lay the cheese on top of the boudin.
5. Starting on 1 side, fold the dough over to the other side forming a long cylinder and seal the ends.
6. Butter a metal baking pan. Place the boudin-stuffed bread on the pan and loop the bread dough to form a circle, folding over the ends.
7. Brush the top of the bread generously with melted butter.
8. Bake for approximately 30 minutes and remove from oven.
9. If using the cane syrup and cracklin topping, pour a thin layer of cane syrup over the bread and sprinkle with cracklin crumbs and green onions.
10. For the pepper jelly and bacon topping, spread pepper jelly over bread and sprinkle with bacon bits.
11. Bake for another 10 minutes or until golden brown. Remove from the oven.
12. Add additional cane syrup and cracklin or pepper jelly and bacon bits.
13. Let cool slightly, slice and serve.

CRAWFISH KING CAKE

Serves: 10 to 12

This one will be the hit of any Mardi Gras party. If using crawfish tails left over from boil, you can skip steps 2 to 4.

12 ounces crawfish tails

½ teaspoon liquid crab boil (optional)

Tony Chachere's seasoning, to taste

¼ cup butter

½ cup onion, chopped

¼ cup bell pepper, chopped

¼ cup celery, chopped

8 ounces cream cheese, softened

2 (8 ounce) packages refrigerated crescent rolls

6 heaping tablespoons Parmesan cheese

food coloring

1. Preheat oven to 375 degrees.

2. If using pre-packaged crawfish tails, place tails in a skillet over medium heat, season with crab boil and Tony Chachere's.

3. Cook for approximately 5 minutes or until tails start to curl up.

4. Drain any liquid that accumulates and set tails aside.

5. Melt butter in skillet over medium heat; sauté onion, bell pepper and celery until translucent, approximately 5 minutes.

6. Reduce heat to low. Stir in cream cheese until melted.

7. Stir in crawfish tails, combine well.

Sarah Chauvin

ASSEMBLY

1. To assemble king cake, unroll crescent dough, separating dough into 16 triangles.

2. Arrange 11 crescent rolls in a circle on a large round baking stone with wide ends of triangles towards the center.

3. The skinny points of the triangles will extend outward and hang over the edge of the stone for now. Wide ends should overlap slightly.

4. Arrange the remaining 5 crescent rolls in the center with wide ends matching up to the wide ends of the outer ring. The skinny points will overlap in the middle for now.

5. Spoon crawfish filling into the dough in a circle on top of the overlapping wide ends.

6. Fold skinny points over the filling and tuck them under the wide section.

7. Continue overlapping the points and tucking until all filling is covered and you have a ring of filled dough resembling a king cake.

8. Bake for 18 to 25 minutes or until king cake is lightly browned on top.

TOPPING

1. To make colored cheese, place 2 heaping tablespoons of grated Parmesan cheese in 3 separate bowls.

2. Add food coloring to tint cheese purple, green and yellow.

3. Using the back of a spoon, stir cheese until all is tinted the desired color.

4. To decorate, sprinkle cheese over baked king cake, alternating purple, green and yellow.

MUFFALETTAS

Serves: 10 to 12

Keep these warm by leaving them wrapped in foil until ready to eat.
Also, great for tailgates!

1 loaf French bread

½ jar of Italian olive salad (recommend Boscoli)

7 slices of hard salami, thinly sliced

½ pound honey ham, thinly sliced

½ pound oven roasted turkey, thinly sliced

12 slices of provolone cheese

1. Preheat oven to 350 degrees.
2. Cut French bread lengthwise.
3. Spread olive salad on top half of loaf.
4. On bottom half of loaf, layer salami, ham, turkey and provolone cheese.
5. Close sandwich and wrap tightly in aluminum foil.
6. Bake in oven in for approximately 30 minutes or until cheese melts. Can be made ahead, wrapped in foil and heated before serving.

Jeanne Peltier Chiasson

SKINNY HURRICANE FOR A CROWD

Serves: 8 drinks

Crowd pleaser that doesn't pack all the calories of a traditional hurricane drink.

2 cups white rum

3 cups light orange juice

3 cups light cranberry juice

orange peel, to garnish

cherries, to garnish

1. Mix rum and juices.
2. Serve over ice, garnish with orange peel and cherry.

Stephanie Toups

KING CAKE MARTINI

Serves: 1 drink

For a festive presentation, garnish the martini glass rim with purple, green and gold sugar.

CINNAMON SIMPLE SYRUP

(makes approximately 8 ounces)
make 1 day ahead minimum,
can store in refrigerator

½ cup sugar

½ cup hot water

2 to 3 cinnamon sticks

MARTINI

3 ounces vodka

1 ounce heavy whipping cream

1 tablespoon brown sugar

1 ounce cinnamon simple syrup

colored sugar (optional)

ground cinnamon, to garnish

1. To make the cinnamon simple syrup, stir sugar and hot water until sugar is completely dissolved.

2. Add cinnamon sticks to mixture and let sit overnight (or until desired flavor is reached) in a closed jar or bottle.

3. To make martini, combine vodka, whipping cream, brown sugar and cinnamon simple syrup in a shaker with ice and shake well.

4. If desired, decorate rim of chilled martini glass with purple, green and gold sugar.

5. Strain drink into glass and top with cinnamon.

Donner-Peltier Distillers

PASTALAYA

Serves: 20

Cooking for more than 20 people? This recipe can easily be increased by adding more meat, and for every pound of pasta, add 1 quart of water.

2 pounds Boston butt pork, cubed

2 to 3 tablespoons season-all

1 to 2 teaspoon(s) olive oil

1 onion, chopped

1 bell pepper, chopped

3 stalks celery, chopped

2 pounds smoked sausage, sliced

1 (10 ounce) can original Rotel

1 (10.5 ounce) can cream of mushroom soup

1 to 2 tablespoon(s) Kitchen Bouquet

1 pound boneless chicken thighs, cut into pieces

2 quarts water

salt and pepper, to taste

2 pounds pasta

3 green onions, chopped

1. Season cubed pork with approximately 1 tablespoon of season-all.

2. Brown pork, in olive oil, in an 8 quart pot on medium high heat until tender, approximately 30 minutes.

3. Add onion, bell pepper and celery and cook down for approximately 10 minutes.

4. Add sausage and cook until browned.

5. Add Rotel, cream of mushroom soup, Kitchen Bouquet for color and another tablespoon of season-all and mix well.

6. Add chicken and simmer until cooked through.

7. Add water and bring to boil. Boil for approximately 5 minutes.

8. Taste for spice and salt. It should be salty and spicy because the addition of pasta will absorb seasoning. Add more if needed.

9. Add pasta. Continue stirring until most of the water has cooked out, approximately 15 to 20 minutes.

10. Turn heat off, add green onions and cover for 20 minutes.

11. Once done take cover off and stir well.

Kyle Bourgeois

HOMEMADE KING CAKE

Serves: 10 to 12

Fun to make with the kids during the Mardi Gras break.

DOUGH

¾ cup milk

¼ cup margarine

3 ¼ cups flour, divided

1 (0.25 ounce) package instant fast-acting yeast

¼ cup sugar

½ teaspoon salt

¼ cup water

1 egg

CINNAMON FILLING

1 cup brown sugar

1 tablespoon cinnamon

½ cup margarine

CREAM CHEESE PECAN FILLING (OPTIONAL)

1 (8 ounce) package cream cheese

½ cup powdered sugar

1 teaspoon vanilla extract

¼ cup butter

pecans, to taste

FRUIT FILLING (OPTIONAL)

2 cups fresh fruit of choice

¼ cup sugar

1 tablespoon cornstarch

1 tablespoon lemon juice

¼ cup water

GLAZE AND TOPPING

3 cups powdered sugar

2 tablespoons butter

2 tablespoons lemon juice

¼ teaspoon vanilla extract

½ cup milk

1/3 cup each purple, green, gold sugar

1. Preheat oven to 375 degrees.
2. Heat milk in microwave for 45 seconds then add margarine and stir to melt.
3. In a separate bowl, combine 2 ¼ cups flour, yeast, sugar, salt and mix well.
4. Add water, egg and warm milk, beat well.
5. Add the remaining flour a little at a time, stirring well after each addition.
6. Cover dough and let rise for approximately 10 minutes.
7. Roll dough into a 22 x 12 inch rectangle. Spread cinnamon filling mixture over rectangular dough.
8. If desired, spread cream cheese pecan filling or fruit filling on top of cinnamon mixture.
9. Roll up dough, mold into a circle and pinch seams to close.
10. Cover and let rise for approximately 30 minutes.
11. Bake for 20 minutes on a greased baking sheet.
12. Make glaze by combining powdered sugar, butter, lemon juice, vanilla extract and 1 teaspoon milk, mix well.
13. Continue adding 1 teaspoon milk until glaze is thin enough to pour.
14. Spread glaze over cake.
15. Decorate with purple, green and gold sugar.

Natalie T Broussard

COPYCAT BROWNIES

Serves: 24 to 48 brownies

This is not the original recipe but tastes just like brownies from
Thibodaux's well known, and now closed, City Bakery.

2 (18.3 ounce) boxes fudge brownie mix

1 (1 pound) box powdered sugar

½ bar Crisco shortening, softened

¼ teaspoon almond extract

¼ cup water

pinch of salt

**½ (14 ounce) container of chocolate
fudge icing**

1. Prepare brownie batter according to package instructions.

2. Pour batter into a greased 13 x 9 inch pan and bake for approximately 25 minutes.

3. Once the brownies are cooked, let them cool for 5 to 10 minutes and use a spatula to flatten them.

4. Turn the pan upside down on a piece of wax paper to allow them to continue to cool. Remove pan.

5. To make the icing, use a mixer, combine powdered sugar, Crisco and almond extract in a bowl.

6. Add water and salt, mix together.

7. Add the chocolate icing and combine.

8. Allow the icing mixture to sit and slightly stiffen before placing on brownies.

9. Once the brownies are cool, spread a thin layer of icing over them (while still upside down), then use a pizza cutter to cut the brownies into rectangles. Leftover icing freezes well.

Lovers of City Bakery

CHOCOLATE CHIP COOKIES WITH A TWIST

Serves: 8 to 10

This variation of a classic recipe from the 1982 Louisiana Legacy Cookbook dresses up a favorite cookie with holiday colored sprinkles.

COOKIES

1 cup shortening

1 cup brown sugar

1 cup granulated sugar

2 eggs, well beaten

1 teaspoon vanilla extract

1 ½ cups flour

1 teaspoon salt

1 teaspoon baking soda

3 cups quick-cooking oatmeal

½ cup pecans, chopped (optional)

1 ½ cups chocolate chips

TOPPING

1 cup chocolate chips

1 cup white chocolate chips

Mardi Gras colored sprinkles

1. Preheat oven to 350 degrees.

2. Cream shortening and sugars together.

3. Add eggs and vanilla extract and beat well.

4. In a separate bowl, sift together flour, salt and baking soda and add to the creamed mixture.

5. Add oatmeal, nuts, if desired, and 1 ½ cups chocolate chips, mixing until blended.

6. Drop by tablespoon on lightly greased cookie sheet.

7. Bake for 10 minutes. Let cool.

8. In a medium size microwavable bowl, add 1 cup of chocolate chips and heat in the microwave for approximately 1 minute.

9. Stir chocolate and heat in additional 15 second intervals in microwave until chocolate can be stirred smoothly.

10. To melt white chocolate chips, heat on low microwave setting so it will not burn.

11. Dip cookie into melted chocolate and top with sprinkles.

12. Place cookies on parchment paper to set, which may take a couple of hours.

1982 Louisiana Legacy Cookbook

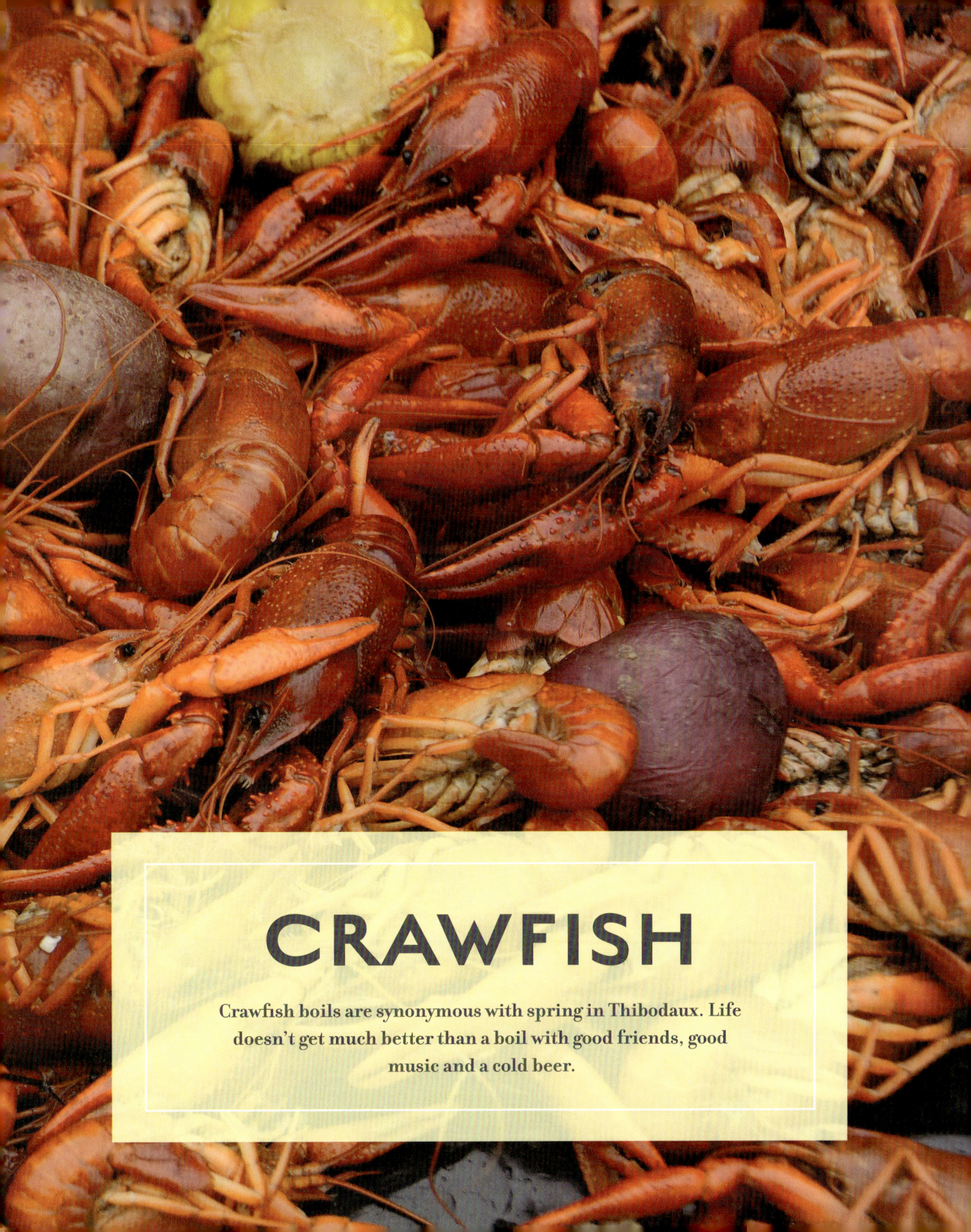

CRAWFISH

Crawfish boils are synonymous with spring in Thibodaux. Life doesn't get much better than a boil with good friends, good music and a cold beer.

BOILED CRAWFISH

Serves: A crowd

Let your out of town guests have the first batch and you wait for the second spicier batch. Citrus flavoring is key to this recipe.

1 to 2 (35 pound) sack(s) of crawfish

1 to 2 (26 ounce) container(s) salt

FIRST BATCH

80 to 100 gallon boil pot

1 (4.5 pound) container Zatarain's extra spicy Crawfish, Shrimp and Crab Boil

1 (8 ounce) bottle lemon liquid crab boil

3 (3 ounce) bags Zatarain's Crawfish, Shrimp and Crab Boil

1 pound bag of potatoes

4 heads garlic

6 large onions

6 large lemons, halved

2 links of your favorite sausage

1 sack crawfish

2 artichokes

1 (10 ounce) carton button mushrooms

1 (12 count) pack frozen corn

ice

PREPARATION

1. Pour crawfish into a large ice chest and cover generously with salt to purge.

2. Add enough water to cover crawfish and allow them to move around.

3. Drain and repeat the process until water is clear.

4. Rinse crawfish and set aside in the shade.

BOIL

1. Fill boil pot ¹⁄₃ of the way full with water.

2. In boil basket, add crab boil, lemon liquid crab boil, crab boil in a bag, potatoes, garlic, onions, lemons and sausage and cover.

3. Bring water to a rolling boil over a high heat propane burner.

4. When water comes to a boil, set a timer and let boil for 5 minutes.

5. Add crawfish and artichokes, bring back to boil, cover and set timer to boil for additional 2 minutes.

6. After 2 minutes, add mushrooms and corn, cover and boil for 5 additional minutes.

7. Turn off propane tank, cover crawfish with ice and soak for 7 minutes, leaving pot uncovered.

8. Carefully remove boil basket from pot and dump onto newspaper covered table.

9. Serve with seafood boil dipping sauce.

10. Reserve seasoned water in pot if doing additional batches.

Jason Higgins

SECOND BATCH

½ (4.5 pound) container of regular Zatarain's Crawfish, Shrimp and Crab Boil

1 (8 ounce) bottle lemon liquid crab boil

3 (3 ounce) bags Zatarain's Crawfish, Shrimp and Crab Boil

1 pound bag of potatoes

4 heads garlic

6 large onions

6 large lemons, halved

2 links of your favorite sausage

1 sack crawfish

2 artichokes

1 (10 ounce) carton button mushrooms

1 (12 count) pack frozen corn

ice

1. Using water from first batch, add crab boil, lemon liquid crab boil, crab boil in a bag, potatoes, garlic, onions, lemons and sausage and cover.

2. Bring water to a rolling boil over a high heat propane burner.

3. When water comes to a boil, set timer and let boil for 5 minutes.

4. Add crawfish and artichokes, bring back to boil, cover and set timer to boil for additional 2 minutes.

5. After 2 minutes, add mushrooms and corn, cover and boil for 5 additional minutes.

6. Turn off propane tank, cover crawfish with ice and soak for 7 minutes, leaving pot uncovered.

7. Carefully remove boil basket from pot and dump onto newspaper covered table.

8. Serve with seafood boil dipping sauce.

9. Reserve seasoned water in pot if doing additional batches and use recipe ingredients from second batch.

SEAFOOD BOIL DIPPING SAUCE

Serves: 4 to 6

1 cup ketchup

½ cup mayonnaise

2 tablespoons horseradish

2 dashes Worcestershire sauce

1. Mix all ingredients together in large bowl.

2. Separate into ramekins or small bowls and serve with boiled seafood.

Jeanne Glaser Higgins

CHEF RYAN GAUDET

HOMETOWN:
Thibodaux, Louisiana

EDUCATION AND EXPERIENCE:
Chef Ryan earned a Bachelor of Science Degree in Culinary Arts from the John Folse Culinary Institute at Nicholls State University. He has worked in numerous restaurants since his sophomore year in high school, including restaurants in Louisiana and high-end restaurants in Chicago. Chef Ryan is now the Executive Chef and on the board of directors at Spahr's Seafood Restaurant. He also serves as a board member of the John Folse Culinary Institute Alumni Chapter.

"Thibodaux is in the heart of bayou country. Surrounded by sugarcane fields and bayous, it's hard not to love the environment and ecosystem that's visible everyday. As a chef, I get to showcase the unique bounties of Louisiana and utilize amazing local products in my dishes. Our Cajun ancestors had to make the most out of the flooded, swampy, almost inhabitable land they were given. Today, Louisiana exports such as crawfish and alligator, raw sugar and rice are enjoyed all over the country and we helped make that possible by following and teaching traditions."

CRAWFISH DEVILED EGGS WITH BACON AIOLI

Serves: 8 to 10

32 eggs (20 for boiling, 12 for the aioli)

2 tablespoons plus 1 teaspoon salt

1 pound crawfish tails

2 tablespoons butter

2 teaspoons Cajun seasoning

1 pound bacon, fat reserved

1 cup vegetable oil

¼ cup lemon juice

1 teaspoon black pepper

1 teaspoon granulated garlic

1 teaspoon cayenne pepper

1 tablespoon Dijon mustard

½ cup green onions, chopped, to garnish

EGGS

1. Place 20 eggs in a pot, cover with water by 1 inch, add 2 tablespoons salt and bring to a boil.

2. When the water starts to boil, lower fire to medium heat and simmer for 8 minutes.

3. Drain the water and add a few cubes of ice to stop the cooking process and to make sure the eggs are cold.

4. Peel, rinse and cut the eggs in half. Remove the cooked yolk and reserve in a mixing bowl.

FILLING

1. Preheat oven to 350 degrees.

2. In a skillet over medium heat, lightly sauté crawfish in butter and Cajun seasoning, just until tails are tender.

3. Using a blender or food processor, chop the crawfish very fine and add to the mixing bowl with the boiled egg yolk.

4. Place bacon on rimmed baking sheet and cook in the oven for 15 minutes or until crispy.

5. Let cool slightly then pour the bacon fat into another pot or bowl and reserve for aioli.

6. You should have approximately 1 cup of bacon fat, add enough vegetable oil so that you have 2 cups total of oil.

7. Chop the bacon.

8. With the remaining 12 eggs, crack and separate the yolks from the whites.

9. Place the yolks in a mixing bowl, add lemon juice, 1 teaspoon salt, pepper, garlic, cayenne pepper and Dijon mustard.

10. Using an electric mixer, whip until it doubles in size or the mixture turns a pale yellow color.

11. With the whip still running, slowly drizzle in the oil/bacon fat.

12. Add the bacon aioli and ½ the chopped bacon to the crawfish mixture. Stir well.

13. Spoon the crawfish and bacon mixture back into the egg halves and garnish with remaining chopped bacon and green onions.

Chef Ryan Gaudet

CRAWFISH BISQUE

Serves: 10 to 12

This dish is a tradition among Louisiana families and is absolutely a labor of love. Best done with mothers and grandmothers to make enough bisque for everyone's freezer.

STUFFING FOR HEADS

2 pounds crawfish tails (with fat)

60 cleaned crawfish heads

2 large onions

2 ribs celery

6 cloves garlic

½ bunch parsley

1 medium bell pepper

2/3 cup butter or bacon fat

½ bunch green onions

1 teaspoon black pepper

1 teaspoon red pepper

1 teaspoon thyme

juice of 1 lemon

1 tablespoon Worcestershire sauce

1 teaspoon monosodium glutamate (optional)

1 tablespoon salt

2 cups seasoned breadcrumbs, divided

1. Preheat oven to 400 degrees.
2. Use leftover crawfish tail meat and cleaned crawfish heads from previous crawfish boil, as well as the fat (can freeze until ready to make bisque).
3. Use remaining leftover shells from crawfish boil to make stock for the bisque.
4. To make stuffing; grind or roughly puree onions, celery, garlic, parsley and bell pepper.
5. Cook in butter or bacon fat until tender.
6. Remove from heat.
7. Grind or roughly puree crawfish tails and green onions and add to above ingredients.
8. Stir in black pepper, red pepper, thyme, lemon juice, Worcestershire sauce, monosodium glutamate, if desired, and salt, mix well.
9. Add 1 ½ cups breadcrumbs a little at a time to make stuffing the proper consistency for handling.
10. Stuff heads and on a flat surface and then roll in remaining ½ cup breadcrumbs.
11. Bake for 10 to 15 minutes, until lightly browned. Remove and set aside.

Jeanne Glaser Higgins
(Martin Family Recipe)

BISQUE

1 cup vegetable oil

1 cup flour

2 tablespoons tomato paste

3 onions, finely chopped

4 ribs celery, finely chopped

4 cloves garlic, finely chopped

1 bell pepper, finely chopped

3 quarts crawfish or seafood stock (see Appendix)

salt and pepper, to taste

1 tablespoon Worcestershire sauce

1 bay leaf

1 lemon, sliced

1 to 2 pound(s) crawfish tails, cleaned

½ bunch parsley, chopped

½ bunch green onions, chopped

cooked rice

1. Combine vegetable oil and flour in Dutch oven over medium heat, stirring constantly until golden brown roux.

2. Add tomato paste, onions, celery, garlic and bell pepper and cook until tender, approximately 5 to 7 minutes.

3. Slowly stir in 3 quarts of stock and bring to a boil.

4. Add salt and pepper, Worcestershire sauce and bay leaf, lower heat and cook 30 to 40 minutes.

5. Drop in lemon slices, crawfish tails and stuffed heads 10 minutes before serving. Gently stirring occasionally.

6. Mix in parsley and green onions, then immediately serve bisque over hot rice and place a few stuffed heads in each soup bowl.

NATALIE'S AFTER THE BOIL SOUP

Serves: 6 to 8

This is a light tasting soup for an easy weeknight dinner the week after a crawfish boil.

4 tablespoons butter

4 tablespoons flour

2 (32 ounce) boxes of chicken broth or stock

4 red potatoes boiled (not from the crawfish boil), quartered (if using potatoes from boil add 2 cups of water to broth)

2 to 3 cups crawfish tails from crawfish boil, peeled

2 to 3 ears of corn from boil, cut off the cob

1 pint half and half

mushrooms from the boil (optional)

salt and pepper, to taste

Natalie Landry

1. Sauté butter and flour to make pale roux, do not brown, it should be cream colored.

2. Pour in chicken stock slowly, continue to mix and whisk until blended and then bring to a simmer.

3. Add potatoes and most of the crawfish and corn, reserving some for later.

4. Return to simmer.

5. Use stick blender to blend in pot or whisk out lumps as needed.

6. Add the half and half, remaining crawfish, corn and mushrooms, if desired.

7. Season with salt and pepper and cook on low heat for 5 minutes then serve.

AFTER THE BOIL LOADED POTATOES

Serves: 12 to 15

Almost as good as the boil.

2 pounds boiled
  potatoes, peeled

½ cup milk

½ sour cream

½ cup butter, melted

1 pound boiled shrimp

1 pound crabmeat

1 boiled onion, chopped
  in food processor

2 cloves boiled garlic,
  chopped in
  food processor

1 link boiled smoked
  sausage, diced

boiled mushrooms (optional)

2 cups mild Cheddar
  cheese, shredded
  and divided

1. Preheat oven to 350 degrees.

2. In a bowl, mash potatoes with potato masher and add milk, sour cream and butter.

3. Add shrimp, crabmeat, onion, garlic, sausage, mushrooms and 1 cup of cheese and mix.

4. Put in a 9 x 13 inch pan and top with remaining cup of cheese.

5. Bake for 30 minutes.

Beau Brooks

CRAWFISH GRILLED CHEESE

Serves: 2

This Cajun twist of the classic grilled cheese will become a family favorite.

8 to 16 ounces Louisiana crawfish tails

½ teaspoon blackened seasoning

4 tablespoons butter, divided

½ tablespoon garlic, minced

2 green onions, chopped and divided

4 slices of Texas toast

1 tablespoon Spahr's Remoulade sauce (or your favorite remoulade sauce)

4 ounces Havarti cheese, shredded

1. Preheat oven to 350 degrees.
2. Season crawfish with blackened seasoning.
3. Sauté crawfish in 2 tablespoons butter and garlic.
4. Add 1 chopped green onion to the pan 1 minute prior to removing from heat.
5. With the remaining 2 tablespoons, butter slices of bread on both sides.
6. Spread remoulade and add cheese to the top of 2 slices of bread.
7. Place those 2 slices, cheese up, in a separate sauté pan on medium heat.
8. Add crawfish to the top of the cheese as it starts to melt.
9. Top with the remaining slices of bread.
10. Flip once. Finish in the oven for 2 additional minutes.
11. Garnish with remaining green onion.

Spahr's Seafood

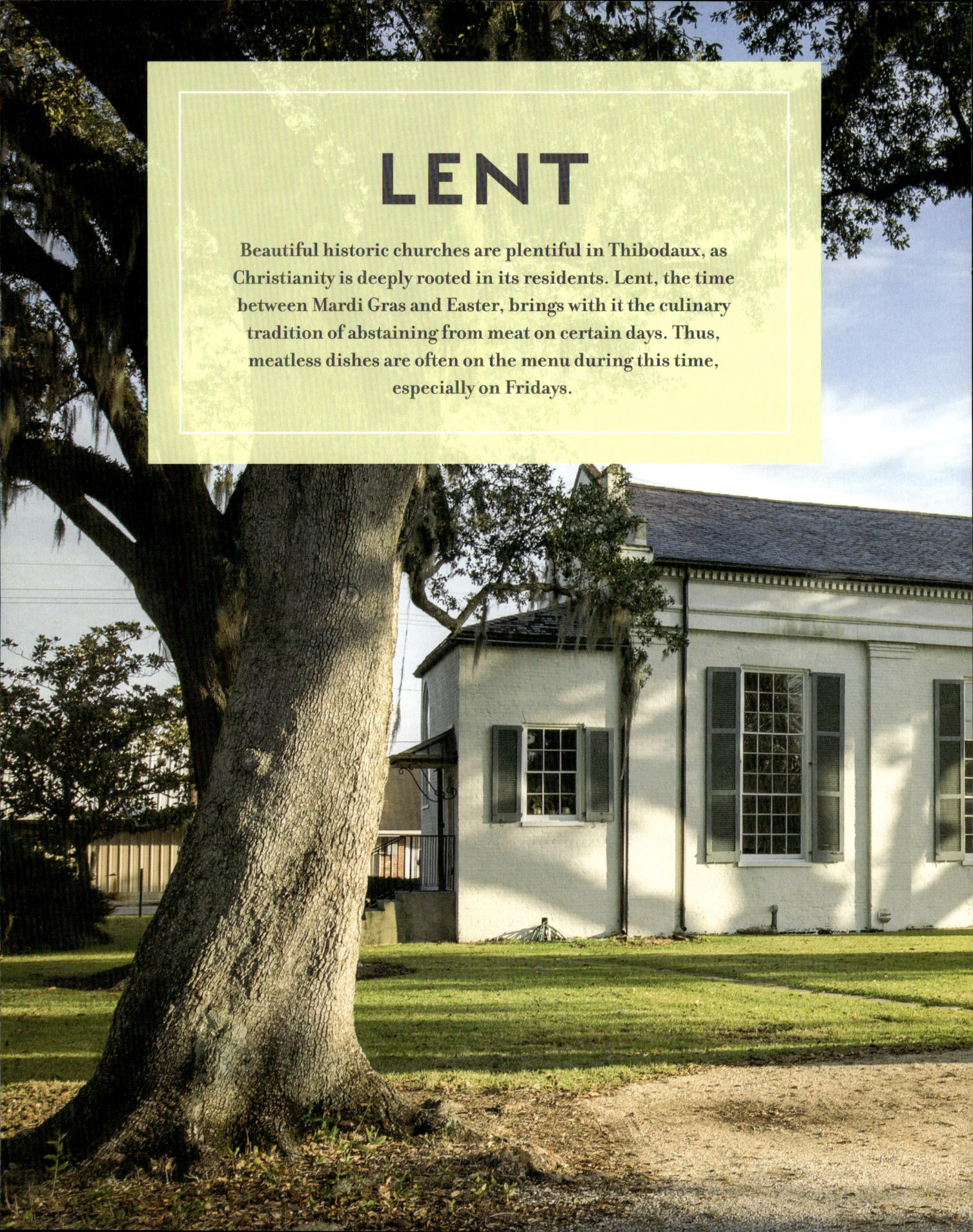

LENT

Beautiful historic churches are plentiful in Thibodaux, as Christianity is deeply rooted in its residents. Lent, the time between Mardi Gras and Easter, brings with it the culinary tradition of abstaining from meat on certain days. Thus, meatless dishes are often on the menu during this time, especially on Fridays.

HOMEMADE FRENCH BREAD

Serves: 24

If you use regular all-purpose flour, add an extra cup of flour.
Regular all-purpose flour makes a softer bread like a roll.

2 packets active yeast

3 cups lukewarm water, approximately 105 to 115 degrees

¼ cup sugar

1/3 cup olive oil

1 tablespoon of salt

6 to 7 cups unbleached ground white wheat flour

Craig Perque

1. In a large bowl, dissolve yeast in warm water and sugar.
2. Let it ferment for approximately 10 to 15 minutes.
3. Add oil, salt and flour. Use 6 cups of the flour to start.
4. Mix together and knead until all ingredients are blended well.
5. The dough will be sticky, elastic like, and will begin to come away from the bowl.
6. Continue to knead and add more flour as needed until the dough stays away from the side of the bowl.
7. With a towel or plastic wrap keep dough covered in a warm area and let rise until the dough doubles in size, approximately 1 to 2 hours.
8. Can preheat oven to the lowest setting then turn off and place covered dough inside.
9. After it doubles in size, punch the dough and divide in 2 halves.
10. Place each half in a greased sheet pan.
11. Cover sheet pan and let rise again until it's over the top of the pan.
12. Place a pan with approximately 1 inch of water in the bottom of the oven to help keep the bread moist.
13. Bake dough at 375 degrees for approximately 20 to 30 minutes or until top of loaf is brown.
14. Remove bread from pan to cool and rub butter over the top of the loaf to give extra brown color.

CHADRON "BULL THISTLE" SPRING SALAD

Serves: 8 to 10

Traditionally in season the week between Palm Sunday and Easter Sunday, the thistle that grows in local Lafourche and Terrebonne Parish pastures is Cirsium horridulum, also known as the Yellow Thistle or Bull Thistle. The stalk is used in this recipe, but if you wait until the flowers bloom and they begin to release their seed heads like a dandelion, you can also eat the seeds, like sunflower seeds.

6 stalks of thistle

1 gallon water

½ teaspoon salt

1 (8 ounce) bag spinach

2 cucumbers, cut into ½ inch cubes

4 plum tomatoes, cut into ½ inch cubes

¼ cup raisins

2 large avocados, chopped into ½ inch cubes

6 ounces feta cheese, crumbled

1 ounce shelled sunflower seeds

1/3 cup Italian salad dressing

1. Send kids out to collect 6 stalks of thistle that have diameters less than 1 inch.

2. Using a steak knife, like whittling wood, trim off the thorny leaves and flowers of the thistle. Save some flowers for the centerpiece.

3. Continue using the same knife to scrape the purple skin off of the stalk, until it is mostly green.

4. Cut the thistle into thin cross section rings, 1/3 inch thick.

5. The most tender parts are near the top of the thistle. The tougher parts are near the base.

6. Soak thistle rings in a gallon of tap water plus salt, while preparing other ingredients.

7. Rinse spinach and add to a large ceramic bowl purchased from a Nicholls Pottery Sale.

8. Add cucumbers, tomatoes, raisins, avocado, feta and sunflower seeds.

9. Remove thistle from water, pat dry and add to salad.

10. Sprinkle with dressing and mix.

11. Serve with thistle flowers in a vase as a centerpiece.

Dr. Gary LaFleur, Jr. and Dr. Jane Carlson,
Center for Bayou Studies at
Nicholls State Univesity

SEAFOOD GUMBO

Serves: 8 to 10

Seafood gumbo is the go-to lunch in Thibodaux for Fridays during Lent and is often sold at local area churches.

2 tablespoons cooking oil

3 large onions, chopped

2 large bell peppers, chopped

4 stalks celery, chopped

2 teaspoons garlic, minced

1 (5 ounce) jar roux (light or dark)

64 ounces shrimp or seafood stock (see Appendix)

20 ounces okra, chopped (fresh or frozen)

24 ounces water, add more if thinner consistency desired

4 pounds shrimp, peeled and deveined

1 tablespoon salt

1 ½ teaspoons garlic powder

1 ½ teaspoons onion powder

1 tablespoon seasoned salt

1 tablespoon liquid crab boil

dash of Louisiana Hot Sauce

2 pounds crabmeat (lump or claw)

½ cup green onions, chopped

¼ cup parsley, chopped

cooked rice

crab claws, to garnish

1. In a large stock pot, heat cooking oil and sauté onions, bell pepper, celery and garlic.
2. Push seasonings to the sides of the pot then add roux in the middle.
3. Over a low fire, melt the roux then mix with seasonings.
4. Add shrimp or seafood stock slowly until well blended.
5. Add okra.
6. Slowly stir in water then add 3 pounds of shrimp (saving 1 pound to add with crabmeat).
7. Season with salt, garlic powder, onion powder, seasoned salt, crab boil and Louisiana Hot Sauce.
8. Cook for 1 to 1 ½ hours over a low fire.
9. Add crabmeat, remaining shrimp, green onions and parsley and let cook for another 30 minutes.
10. Avoid stirring gumbo too much so crabmeat does not break apart.
11. Serve over hot rice.
12. Garnish with boiled crab claws.

Kristi B Gravois

POTATO SALAD

Serves: 8 to 10

No gumbo is complete without a side of potato salad.

3 pounds red potatoes

6 eggs

2 tablespoons salt

½ cup mayonnaise

3 tablespoons mustard

salt and pepper, to taste

2 tablespoons fresh parsley, chopped (optional)

½ cup celery, finely chopped (optional)

1. Place potatoes, eggs and 2 tablespoons of salt in a large pot of water.
2. Boil until tender, approximately 15 to 20 minutes.
3. Drain the potatoes and set aside to cool.
4. Peel and chop eggs.
5. Peel potatoes and quarter.
6. Combine potatoes, eggs, mayonnaise, mustard and salt and pepper, to taste.
7. If desired, add parsley and celery.
8. Mix until blended to desired consistency.

Jeanne Glaser Higgins

LENTEN TOMATO GRAVY AND EGGS

Serves: 6 to 8

For a lighter version, try with just egg whites.

1 large onion, chopped

1 medium bell pepper, chopped

2 stalks celery, chopped

1 tablespoon oil

2 (14.5 ounce) cans original stewed tomatoes, blended into small pieces

1 (6 ounce) can tomato paste

1 (15 ounce) can tomato sauce

2 to 3 cups water

salt and pepper, to taste

14 raw eggs

cooked rice

1. In a Dutch oven, sauté onion, bell pepper and celery over medium heat in oil until translucent.

2. Add stewed tomatoes, tomato paste and tomato sauce, stirring well.

3. Add water to mixture, approximately 2 to 3 cups, or until the sauce is the desired thickness.

4. Bring the mixture to a boil and simmer for 1 hour.

5. Add water as needed to thin sauce.

6. Add salt and pepper to taste.

7. Crack raw eggs into individual bowls and carefully add to tomato sauce 1 at a time, without breaking the yolk.

8. Do not stir.

9. Cover and cook for approximately 20 to 25 minutes.

10. Serve over hot rice.

Gayle Toups Thibodaux, in memory of Una Mae "Felo" Toups

CRAWFISH AND SHRIMP STEW

Serves: 8 to 10

*Father Carlos often serves this dish for friends and his brother
Catholic priests in the Houma-Thibodaux Diocese.*

½ cup oil

½ cup flour

1 onion, finely chopped

3 stalks celery, finely chopped

1 bell pepper, finely chopped

½ cup water

2 (12 ounce) packages fresh crawfish tails

1 pound shrimp, cleaned and peeled

1 can Rotel

salt and pepper, to taste

cooked rice

hot sauce (optional)

boiled eggs, peeled and sliced (optional)

bell pepper, thinly cut and sliced
  lengthwise (optional)

1. Combine oil and flour in Dutch oven over medium heat.
2. Stir constantly until roux has the color and texture of creamy peanut butter.
3. Add onion, celery and bell pepper and sauté.
4. Cover and cook for 30 minutes on low to medium heat.
5. Stir occasionally and add water, careful not to burn.
6. Add crawfish tails and shrimp and cook until shrimp turn pink.
7. Add Rotel and salt and pepper to taste.
8. Cover and cook for 30 to 45 minutes.
9. Serve with hot rice and optional garnishes; hot sauce, boiled eggs or bell pepper.

Reverend Carlos Talavera

CAJUN SHRIMP ROTINI

Serves: 8 to 10

2 ½ sticks of butter

1 cup onion, chopped

1 tablespoon garlic, minced

1 to 2 tablespoon(s) Tony
   Chachere's seasoning

1 tablespoon Worcestershire sauce

1 tablespoon fresh basil, chopped

1 tablespoon fresh thyme, chopped

3 tablespoons fresh parsley, chopped

2 pounds Louisiana gulf shrimp (40 to 50
   count), peeled and deveined

1 (16 ounce) package rotini pasta, cooked

8 ounces Velveeta cheese, cubed

1. Preheat oven to 350 degrees.

2. In a large skillet, add butter and sauté onion and garlic for approximately 8 minutes.

3. Add Tony Chachere's, Worcestershire sauce, basil, thyme and parsley.

4. In a 13 x 9 inch baking dish, evenly layer shrimp and top with cooked vegetable mixture.

5. Bake for 25 minutes stirring occasionally.

6. Add cooked Rotini pasta and Velveeta cheese, stir to combine.

7. Bake for an additional 10 minutes or until cheese is melted.

Beau Brooks

GRILLED RACK OF LAMB

Serves: 2 to 4

Great for a Passover meal or any day of the year.

1 rack of lamb

salt, to taste

2 tablespoons rosemary, finely minced

2 to 3 cloves garlic, finely minced

2 to 3 tablespoons olive oil

1. Cut rack of lamb into 2 bones per piece and bring to room temperature.
2. Salt both sides.
3. Pulverize rosemary and garlic with a mortar and pestle, add olive oil until it forms a thick consistency.
4. Spread rosemary mixture on both sides of the lamb.
5. Grill over medium heat.
6. Lamb is done when internal temperature reaches 135 degrees.
7. Let rest 5 minutes prior to serving.
8. To serve, cut each double chop into "popsicles."

Paul Cummins

EASTER BRUNCH

This beautiful table and menu to match are perfect for celebrating Easter morning with family and friends. Your guests will be wowed from seafood start to the chocolate-filled finish. This menu also works seamlessly for other spring happenings such as bridal showers, Mother's Day, graduations and First Communions.

— MENU —

SKINNY CAJUN CRAB CAKES, CRAWFISH BENNY,
VIDALIA ONION TARTE

SKINNY MILK PUNCH,
ANNIE MANNIE'S CHAMPAGNE SHERBET PUNCH

TRADITIONAL SOUTHERN GRILLADES,
CHEESE PLANTATION BISCUITS, JAZZED UP GRITS,
BLUEBERRY JALAPENO SALAD

CADBURY EGG BREAD PUDDING,
GERMAN CHOCOLATE CHIP CAKE,
GIRL SCOUT THIN MINT PIE,
GIRL SCOUT PEANUT BUTTER PATTY DIP

SKINNY CAJUN CRAB CAKES

Serves: 6 crab cakes

These crab cakes were a part of the dish that won the Eat Fit NOLA cook-off in 2017.

1 pound jumbo lump crab meat

¼ cup breadcrumbs

1 tablespoon Dijon mustard

1 tablespoon creole mustard

1 egg, beaten

1/8 teaspoon crab boil

½ cup red or white onion (not yellow), finely chopped

¼ cup parsley, finely chopped

salt, to taste

1. Preheat oven to 400 degrees.
2. Mix all ingredients and let chill for 30 minutes in fridge.
3. From into 6 patties or 12 bites and place on greased cookie sheet.
4. Bake for 7 minutes.

Craig Perque

CRAWFISH BENNY

Serves: 10 to 12

A unique and memorable dip—especially for crawfish lovers.

1 cup butter

2 to 3 tablespoons flour

3 cloves garlic, chopped

6 drops Kitchen Bouquet

¼ cup pimentos, chopped

2 (4 ounce) cans mushrooms, sliced
   and drained (optional)

2 ½ to 3 pounds crawfish tails

2/3 bunch parsley, chopped

1 bunch green onions, chopped

1 (5 ounce) can water chestnuts, sliced
   and drained

salt, to taste

red pepper, to taste

1. Melt butter in large skillet over low heat.
2. Sprinkle in flour and stir until blended.
3. Add garlic, Kitchen Bouquet, pimentos and mushrooms.
4. Sauté 3 to 4 minutes.
5. Mix in crawfish tails and cook 15 to 20 minutes, stirring continuously.
6. Stir in parsley, green onions and water chestnuts.
7. Cook 3 to 4 minutes until flavors blend.
8. Season with salt and red pepper to taste.
9. Serve this dip hot with assorted crackers.

1982 Louisiana Legacy Cookbook

VIDALIA ONION TARTE

Serves: 6 to 8

An easy recipe that looks and tastes gourmet.

2 tablespoons butter

5 (approximately 4 to 5 cups) small
   Vidalia onions, thinly sliced

2 teaspoons fresh rosemary, chopped

¾ teaspoon salt

½ teaspoon pepper

1 refrigerated pie crust

parchment paper

1 egg white, slightly beaten

¾ cup grated Gruyere cheese, divided

1. Preheat oven to 425 degrees.

2. In a large skillet, over medium high heat, melt butter and add onions along with rosemary, salt and pepper.

3. Cook, stirring occasionally until tender, approximately 7 to 8 minutes.

4. Unroll pie crust onto a lightly floured surface, roll or pat into a 12 inch circle.

5. Transfer pie crust onto a parchment paper lined baking sheet.

6. Brush with egg white. Add half of cheese to center of crust.

7. Spoon onion mixture over cheese, leaving a 2 to 3 inch border.

8. Sprinkle remaining cheese over onions and fold pie crust border up and over onion, crimping as you go, leaving a 4 inch opening in the center.

9. Brush the crust with egg whites.

10. Bake on the bottom rack for 18 to 20 minutes, or until crust is golden.

11. Let stand for 5 to 10 minutes before serving.

Anne Rodrigue

SKINNY MILK PUNCH

Serves: 1 drink

A red hot cocktail!

1 ounce Fireball Cinnamon Whiskey

2 ounces Rum Chata

1 ounce white rum

¼ to ½ cup vanilla soy milk

cinnamon, to garnish

1. Fill a shaker with ice. Add Fireball Cinnamon Whiskey, Rum Chata and white rum.
2. Fill remainder of shaker with vanilla soy milk.
3. Shake.
4. Poor over ice and garnish with cinnamon.

Ashley M Raynal

ANNIE MANNIE'S CHAMPAGNE SHERBERT PUNCH

Serves: 30 to 40

To change the color of the punch, use a different flavor Jello mix.

3 cups sugar

2 cups water

2 (3 ounce) boxes of strawberry Jello

3 quarts cold water, divided

1 (12 ounce) can frozen lemonade

1 (12 ounce) can frozen orange juice

1 (46 ounce) can pineapple juice

1 tablespoon almond extract

2 (2 liter) bottles ginger ale

2 bottles of champagne, or 7-Up

½ to 1 gallon pineapple sherbet

1. In a large saucepan, dissolve sugar in 2 cups boiling water.

2. Keep on low heat. Add Jello and stir until dissolved.

3. Add 1 quart cold water, frozen lemonade, frozen orange juice, pineapple juice and almond extract and stir.

4. Stir in 2 quarts cold water.

5. Place ingredients into 2 plastic containers or punch molds, approximately 3 liters each.

6. If using a smaller punch bowl, adjust sizing of molds.

7. Freeze until solid.

8. When ready to serve, place 1 frozen punch mold in punch bowl and add 1 bottle ginger ale and 1 bottle of champagne.

9. Stir. Punch will become like a slush.

10. Add scoops of sherbet to liquid punch.

11. Add additional mold and bottles of ginger ale and champagne as needed throughout the party.

Jennifer Peltier Wise

TRADITIONAL SOUTHERN GRILLADES

Serves: 8 to 10

A traditional New Orleans dish that is a perfect breakfast for a large group. This recipe uses beef tenderloin trimmings, although the recipe originally calls for cheaper less tender cuts of beef such as chuck, rump or shoulder.

3 pounds beef tenderloin scrap, cut into 1 inch pieces

1 teaspoon kosher salt

½ teaspoon black pepper

½ teaspoon garlic powder

¾ cup seasoned flour, divided

5 slices bacon, chopped

2 tablespoons vegetable oil

½ cup butter

1 red bell pepper, chopped

2 onions, chopped

1 cup celery, chopped

5 large cloves garlic, smashed

5 cups chicken stock

3 bay leaves

1 teaspoon ground basil

2 tablespoons Tabasco sauce

1 tablespoon Worcestershire sauce

5 Roma tomatoes, cubed

½ cup fresh parsley leaves, chopped

1. Season cut beef with salt, pepper and garlic powder, or more to taste. Pound each piece to ½ inch thickness.

2. Toss beef with enough flour to coat, set the remaining flour aside.

3. Render bacon with oil in Dutch oven or large flat-bottomed pot on medium heat to release fat. Remove bacon pieces.

4. Turn heat up to high and brown meat in batches.

5. Remove meat and set aside.

6. Add butter and ½ cup flour and turn down to medium heat to make a brown roux.

7. Add bell pepper, onions, celery and garlic and cook until soft.

8. Return meat and bacon to pot and add chicken stock, bay leaves, basil, Tabasco sauce and Worcestershire sauce.

9. Cook for 1 to 2 hours or until meat is tender and sauce has thickened.

10. Add tomatoes and parsley and turn off heat.

11. Serve over hot grits.

Chef Lindsay R Mason

CHEESE PLANTATION BISCUITS

Serves: 15 to 20

This variation from the original calls for the addition of Cheddar cheese. But they are still delicious in their original form too.

2 ½ cups flour

1 ½ tablespoons baking powder

½ teaspoon salt

2 tablespoons sugar

¾ cup solid shortening

2/3 cup milk

1 ½ cups sharp Cheddar cheese, shredded

1. Preheat oven to 400 degrees.
2. In a bowl, mix flour, baking powder, salt and sugar.
3. Cut in shortening with a pastry blender or knife and fork until mixture is in pea-size granules.
4. Add milk until dough holds together.
5. Sprinkle board with flour and knead dough lightly several times.
6. Sprinkle dough well with flour and roll out to ¾ inch thickness.
7. Knead in shredded cheese.
8. Cut with a 2 inch cutter and bake on an ungreased cookie sheet for 10 to 20 minutes or until golden brown.

Based on 1982 Louisiana Legacy Cookbook

JAZZED UP GRITS

Serves: 4 to 6

A sausage entrée is complemented nicely by this dish. It will ruin your diet, but it's worth it.

2 cups uncooked hominy grits

6 ounces Velveeta or shredded Cheddar cheese

1 cup butter

¼ bunch green onions, minced

dash of Tabasco sauce

2 eggs

1 cup milk

½ teaspoon garlic salt

¼ cup Cheddar cheese, grated

1. Preheat oven to 350 degrees.
2. Make grits according to package and season to taste.
3. Pour warm grits into a bowl add 6 ounces of cheese and butter, stir and set aside to melt.
4. Fold in onions and Tabasco sauce, stir well.
5. In a 1 cup measuring cup, beat eggs and fill to the top with milk.
6. Add egg mixture and garlic salt to the grits and stir.
7. Pour mixture into a buttered, 2 quart casserole dish.
8. Bake for 45 minutes.
9. Top with ¼ cup grated Cheddar cheese and bake another 15 minutes, until bubbly and lightly browned.

1982 Louisiana Legacy Cookbook

BLUEBERRY JALAPENO SALAD

Serves: 6 to 8

Interesting combination of ingredients that come together to make a delicious dish.

2 seedless English cucumbers, halved lengthwise, and sliced into half moons

1 teaspoon salt

1 large jalapeno, finely chopped, seeds and ribs discarded

4 teaspoons fresh lime juice

1 clove garlic, finely chopped

¼ teaspoon ground cumin

¼ cup extra virgin olive oil

1 ½ pints blueberries

1 cup cilantro leaves

1. Season sliced cucumbers with salt.
2. In a large bowl, combine jalapeno, lime juice, garlic and cumin with the extra virgin olive oil and stir.
3. Add the cucumbers, blueberries and cilantro and toss to coat.
4. Chill and serve immediately.

Brandi M Westbrook

CADBURY EGG BREAD PUDDING

Serves: 10 to 12

This Easter spin on classic bread pudding is quick to make and easy enough to have your kids help.

1 loaf of French bread, cut into
   1 inch pieces

5 eggs, lightly beaten

1 ¼ cups milk

1 ¼ cups heavy whipping cream

1/3 cup superfine sugar

1 teaspoon vanilla extract

24 Cadbury mini creme eggs, halved

ICING

3 cups powdered sugar

¼ cup milk

1 teaspoon vanilla extract

1. Preheat oven to 350 degrees.
2. Arrange bread pieces on to a greased 13 x 9 inch baking dish.
3. Whisk together the eggs, milk, cream, sugar and vanilla extract then pour evenly over the bread.
4. Top with halved creme eggs.
5. Bake in oven for 20 to 30 minutes or until set.
6. Allow to cool slightly before serving.
7. To make icing, whisk powdered sugar, milk and vanilla together.
8. Pour over warm bread pudding.

Chef John Folse Culinary Institute

GERMAN CHOCOLATE CHIP CAKE

Serves: 10 to 12

2 (8 ounce) bars German chocolate

1 (16.5 ounce) box yellow cake mix

1 (3.4 ounce) package instant vanilla pudding mix

1 cup cooking oil

1 cup milk

2 eggs

1 (12 ounce) package of chocolate chips

¼ cup powdered sugar, sifted

1. Preheat oven to 350 degrees.

2. Grate ¼ cup of German chocolate for topping and set aside.

3. Pulverize the rest of chocolate in a food processor.

4. Combine pulverized chocolate, cake mix, vanilla pudding mix, oil, milk and eggs and mix.

5. Spray the bottom of 9 x 13 inch baking pan and pour mixture into it.

6. Bake for 40 to 50 minutes until toothpick can pierce cleanly.

7. Cool and sprinkle the saved grated chocolate and powdered sugar on the cake and serve.

Barbara Pierson Gauthier

GIRL SCOUT THIN MINT PIE

Serves: 8 to 10

Support our local girl scouts with this one.

1 (11 ounce) box Thin Mint Girl
   Scout Cookies

¼ cup butter, melted

½ gallon mint chocolate chip ice cream

1 jar hot fudge topping

1. Blend cookies in food processor until crumbled.
2. Mix melted butter with cookie crumbles and press into a pie pan to form crust.
3. Place in freezer for 30 minutes.
4. Scoop ice cream into pan and spread over crust.
5. Warm hot fudge and drizzle on top.
6. Freeze for 15 minutes and serve immediately from freezer, using warm knife to cut.

Ashley Becnel

GIRL SCOUT PEANUT BUTTER PATTY DIP

Serves: 8 to 10

This dip is made with one of the all time favorite Girl Scout cookies—peanut butter patties—also known as Tagalong cookies.

8 ounces cream cheese, softened

½ cup peanut butter

2 cups powdered sugar

1 to 2 tablespoon(s) milk

10 Peanut Butter Patty Girl Scout Cookies

1. In a mixer or food processor, combine cream cheese and peanut butter until smooth.

2. Gradually add in powdered sugar and milk, whisking in between additions.

3. Add cookies, mix on high until well incorporated.

4. Serve at room temperature with apples and/or graham crackers.

Ashley Becnel

CAJUN CINCO DE MAYO

Traditional Mexican recipes with added Cajun flare.

BOUDIN NACHOS

Serves: 4 to 6

A taste tester favorite!

1 (7 ounce) can chipotle peppers in
   adobe sauce

16 ounces sour cream

3 egg roll wrappers

canola oil

1 pound of your favorite boudin, removed
   from casing

8 ounces Gouda cheese, shredded

jalapenos, sliced (optional)

1. Preheat oven to 350 degrees.

2. To make pepper sour cream topping, puree ½ can of chipotle peppers.

3. Mix pureed pepper sauce into sour cream.

4. Add more pepper puree for increased spice.

5. Cut the individual egg roll wrappers into 4 even squares, totaling 12.

6. Heat canola oil to 350 degrees and fry the cut egg roll wrappers for 1 minute on each side, making sure they don't fold up during the frying process.

7. Warm boudin in either a frying pan or in the oven.

8. Lay out 12 fried egg roll squares on a greased pan, top with a spoonful of warm boudin and shredded Gouda cheese.

9. Bake in oven for 5 to 7 minutes or until cheese is completely melted.

10. Top with the sour cream mixture and, if additional spice desired, top with sliced jalapenos.

Ben Malbrough

ROBIN'S FAMOUS MARGARITAS

Serves: 18 to 20

1 (12 ounce) can frozen lemonade

2 (12 ounce) cans frozen limeade

14 ounces Triple Sec

24 ounces Tequila

3 quarts water

1. Mix all ingredients well.
2. Place mixture into freezer safe container(s).
3. Freeze containers, stirring the mixture 1 to 2 times in a 24 hour period.
4. Can be kept in freezer and served when desired, will be a frozen or slushy consistency.

Anne Rodrigue

SPICY SHRIMP TACOS

Serves: 4 to 6

Fried shrimp, fried fish or even grilled red fish work well with this recipe.

3 to 4 Arbol chili peppers

½ cup butter

2 to 3 cloves garlic, chopped

½ teaspoon black pepper

½ teaspoon Mexican oregano

½ teaspoon salt

2/3 cup chicken broth

1 ½ pounds medium shrimp, peeled, deveined and cut into ½ inch pieces

12 flour tortillas

4 ounces Mexican melting cheese or Monterey Jack cheese

1 cup Mexican Spicy Mayo (see recipe below)

bacon, cooked and crumbled (optional)

tomatoes, diced (optional)

1. In a skillet, over medium heat, toast the Arbol peppers until they become aromatic, approximately 1 ½ minutes.
2. Take them out, let cool and crumble.
3. Heat butter in the skillet over medium heat, add garlic and stir for 1 minute.
4. Stir in chili pieces, pepper, oregano, salt and broth.
5. Raise heat to medium high and boil until the mixture has reduced to just a few tablespoons and is noticeably thicker, approximately 8 minutes.
6. Add shrimp and stir until pieces are nearly cooked through, approximately 8 minutes.
7. Remove from heat.
8. To make the tacos, heat 2 tortillas then flip them over.
9. Sprinkle cheese on 1 tortilla then cover with the other and remove from heat.
10. Spread Mexican Spicy Mayo on the topside, add a serving of the spicy shrimp, then, as desired, add more cheese, crumbled bacon and diced tomatoes.
11. Repeat with remaining tortillas. Slice tacos into fourths and serve.

MEXICAN SPICY MAYO

Serves: 4 to 6

3 egg yolks

1 tablespoon lime juice

¾ cup oil

2 to 3 avocados, peeled and pitted

2 to 3 serrano peppers, chopped

¼ cup cilantro, chopped

salt, to taste

1. In a food processor, combine egg yolks and lime juice.
2. While the machine is still running, drizzle in the oil.
3. With the machine off, add the avocado, peppers and cilantro.
4. Let the processor run for 20 to 30 seconds until creamy.
5. If not creamy enough, add more avocado.
6. Add salt and additional lime juice to taste.

David Fournet
Inspired by Rick Bayless

GRILLED STREET CORN

Serves: 4 to 6

Great with sweet summer corn too.

1/3 cup sour cream

1/3 cup mayonnaise

1 clove garlic, minced

½ teaspoon ancho chili powder or regular chili powder, extra to garnish

1 teaspoon lime zest

1 tablespoon lime juice

6 ears of fresh corn, husks peeled back to remove silk

½ cup cotija cheese or Parmesan cheese, grated

½ cup cilantro leaves, roughly chopped

1. Preheat grill to 400 degrees.

2. In a mixing bowl, combine sour cream, mayonnaise, garlic, chili powder, lime zest and juice and mix well.

3. To prepare corn, peel back husks, remove silks and discard.

4. Replace husks to cover corn. If husks are dry, soak in water for 5 minutes prior to placing on grill.

5. Place corn on grill for 4 to 5 minutes, turning once, until charred on each side.

6. Remove from grill, remove husks and coat with sour cream mixture.

7. Top with cheese, cilantro and a pinch of chili powder.

8. Serve immediately.

Christopher and Anne Rodrigue

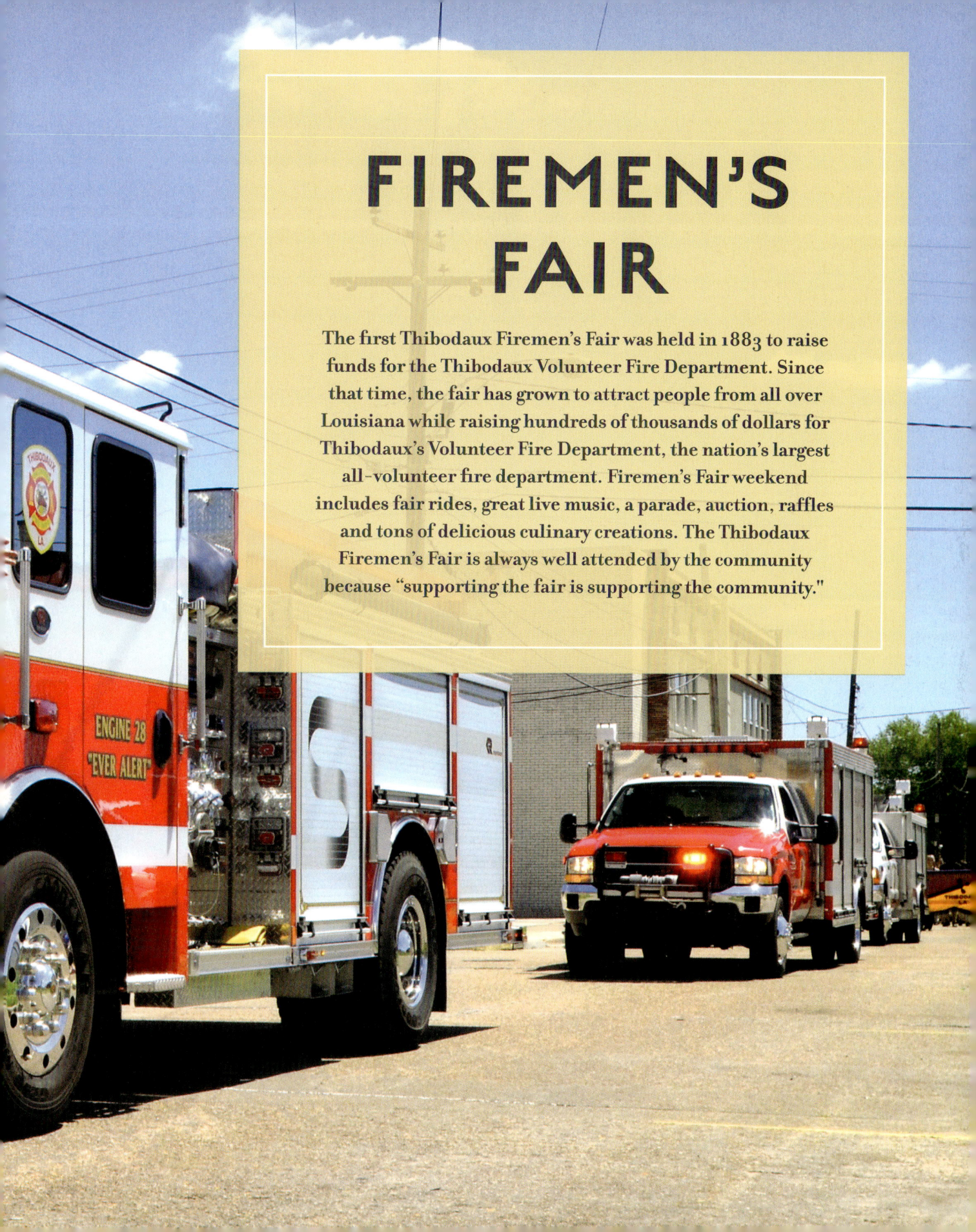

FIREMEN'S FAIR

The first Thibodaux Firemen's Fair was held in 1883 to raise funds for the Thibodaux Volunteer Fire Department. Since that time, the fair has grown to attract people from all over Louisiana while raising hundreds of thousands of dollars for Thibodaux's Volunteer Fire Department, the nation's largest all-volunteer fire department. Firemen's Fair weekend includes fair rides, great live music, a parade, auction, raffles and tons of delicious culinary creations. The Thibodaux Firemen's Fair is always well attended by the community because "supporting the fair is supporting the community."

FAIR CRAWFISH PIES

Serves: 12

The firemen use Keebler tart shells for the crawfish pies at the fair because the sweetness of the tarts compliments the savory filling. Could also make this recipe with a full size pie shell.

1 stick butter

1 cup onions, chopped

1 (10.5 ounce) can cream of mushroom soup

1 pound crawfish tails, peeled

1 (12 ounce) can evaporated milk

1 tablespoon corn starch

2 teaspoons Tony Chachere's seasoning

hot sauce, to taste

¼ cup green onions

1 dozen small tart shells (recommend Keebler)

1. Preheat oven to 350 degrees.

2. In a skillet, melt butter and sauté onions until clear.

3. Add soup and bring mixture to a simmer.

4. Add crawfish tails and bring back to a simmer.

5. In a separate dish, combine evaporated milk and corn starch until thoroughly incorporated and add to soup mixture.

6. Bring back to a simmer.

7. Season with Tony Chachere's and hot sauce.

8. Add green onions and cook at a simmer for 10 minutes.

9. Place mixture in pie shells and bake for 30 minutes or until golden brown.

Walt Lanier

FIREMEN'S FAIR BLOODY MARY BAR

Serves: 8

Can be easily doubled or tripled for a crowd.

1 ½ cups vodka

1 (32 ounce) bottle of Bloody Mary mix
  (recommend Zing Zang)

2 tablespoons lime juice

celery salt, to taste

1. Mix vodka, Bloody Mary mix and lime juice in a large drink dispenser, sprinkle with celery salt.

2. Arrange toppings in a tray.

3. Provide ice filled glasses for guest to fill and have them create their drinks with desired toppings.

TOPPINGS AND GARNISHES

celery sticks

olives

pickles

lime wedges

boiled shrimp

lemon wedges

beef jerky

parsley

pickled green beans

pickled okra

crispy bacon

pickled carrots

pepperoncini

cherry tomatoes

pickled onions

bell pepper strips

Ken and Maria Cruse

FIREMEN'S FAIR BREAKFAST BRANDY MILK PUNCH

Serves: 30

2 bottles (75mL/fifths) brandy

4 cups simple syrup

5 ¾ cups heavy cream

1/3 cup vanilla extract
   (recommend good quality)

nutmeg, to garnish

1. Mix brandy, simple syrup, cream and vanilla extract in a large drink dispenser.

2. Serve over ice and sprinkle with nutmeg.

Ken and Maria Cruse

CHEF NATHAN RICHARD

HOMETOWN:

Thibodaux, Louisiana

EDUCATION AND EXPERIENCE:

Chef Nathan studied at Delgado Culinary Institution in New Orleans. After his training, he worked as a pastry chef at Commander's Palace and at Husk Restaurant in Charleston, South Carolina, under Executive Chef Sean Brock. Chef Nathan then worked for James Beard Award winning Chef Donald Link at Cochon in Lafayette. Next, Nathan moved back to New Orleans and opened Restaurant R'evolution as their lead butcher. He then became Executive Chef at The Bombay Club, followed by tenures in the same position at Kingfish and Cavan Restaurant. Currently, he is the Executive Chef at DTB (Down the Bayou) and was named 2019 King of Louisiana Seafood and 2019 King of American Seafood. He additionally works as an adjunct professor for Nicholls State University in the advanced garde manger and butchering programs and is a Thibodaux volunteer Fireman.

"Thibodaux inspires my ability to be a great chef simply by its surroundings: sugarcane, Bourgeois Meat Market, family gatherings with jambalaya and catfish coubillion. It embodies community centered around strong values and southern hospitality. Being a volunteer fire fighter and teacher at Nicholls State, I have the opportunity to still be active here...even if I'm living in the city now!"

CRAWFISH AND ARTICHOKE GRATIN

Serves: 2 to 4

Can also be served as an appetizer.

2 ounces unsalted butter

½ cup green onion white bottoms, thinly sliced

½ cup yellow onion, chopped

1 cup celery, diced

1 jalapeno, stemmed, seeded and minced

4 cloves garlic, minced

2 bunches green onion tops, chopped

1 teaspoon kosher salt

¼ teaspoon black pepper

1/8 teaspoon cayenne pepper

1 cup artichoke, chopped

2 pounds crawfish tail meat, chopped

½ cup sherry

¼ cup all-purpose flour

1 cup heavy cream

1 squeeze of fresh lemon juice

1 cup white Cheddar cheese, grated

1 cup Parmesan cheese, grated

1 cup French breadcrumbs

1. In a 10 or 12 inch cast iron skillet, melt 2 tablespoons of butter over medium heat.

2. Add green onion white bottoms, yellow onion, celery, jalapeno, garlic, green onion tops, salt, black pepper, cayenne pepper, artichoke and crawfish. Cook, stirring until the vegetables soften, approximately 4 to 6 minutes.

3. Add sherry and continue to simmer until the liquid is reduced by $2/3$, approximately 4 more minutes.

4. Add the flour and cook, stirring, until reduced by about a quarter, approximately 5 minutes.

5. Add the heavy cream. Turn off the heat and stir in the lemon juice and both cheeses.

6. Melt remaining 2 tablespoons of butter and combine with the breadcrumbs in a small bowl.

7. Transfer the crawfish mixture to a 6 x 8 inch baking dish, top with breadcrumbs and broil until the crumbs are nicely browned, 1 to 2 minutes.

Chef Nathan Richard

BUDDY LEDET'S JAMBALAYA

Serves: 8 to 10

2014 Big Boys Cook-off Jambalaya Champion.

1 to 1.5 pound(s) Boston butt pork roast, trimmed and chopped into bite-sized pieces

¼ cup Louisiana Hot Sauce

¼ cup Worcestershire sauce

1 to 2 tablespoon(s) Cajun seasoning, divided

1 pound smoked sausage, cut into ¼ inch thick medallions

1 pound Cajun vegetable trinity

5 ounces canned Rotel tomatoes

2 cups water

2 cups chicken broth

1 pound par-boiled rice

1 tablespoon Kitchen Bouquet

Buddy Ledet

1. Marinate cubed pork in Louisiana Hot Sauce, Worcestershire sauce and 1 tablespoon Cajun seasoning for at least 3 hours.

2. Place pot over medium heat and coat inside of pot with oil or nonstick spray.

3. Add marinated pork and brown over medium heat for approximately 30 minutes or until most of the liquid has cooked out.

4. Add sausage and stir with pork for approximately 5 minutes. If pork and sausage start to stick, add water to prevent sticking.

5. Add Cajun vegetable trinity and Rotel tomatoes and sauté until most of the liquid has cooked out, approximately 20 minutes.

6. Add water, chicken broth and 2 teaspoons Cajun seasoning, adjust to taste.

7. Allow to come to a low boil. Occasionally skimming off any grease from the top and discarding.

8. Add rice and Kitchen Bouquet, stirring continuously until the rice has absorbed enough water to a point that the rice level and water level are almost equal.

9. Cover pot tightly, turn off burner and allow to sit for 40 to 45 minutes.

BOWIE FIRE STATION SHRIMP STEW

Serves: 200 to 300
(made in a 30 gallon jambalaya pot)

Serves: 8 to 10

The first recipe is "fair size." The second is "home size." On a usual Fair weekend, Bowie Fire Station cooks 2 batches each on Saturday and Sunday of the "fair size" stew.

2 gallons vegetable oil	1 cup vegetable oil
16 pounds flour	1 cup flour
20 pounds onions, chopped	1 cup onions, chopped
10 pounds celery, chopped	½ cup celery, chopped
10 pounds bell pepper, chopped	½ cup bell pepper, chopped
15 gallons water	2 quarts chicken stock (add more or less to adjust consistency)
60 pounds (80 count size) shrimp, peeled	
6 heaping cooking spoons hot sauce	2 pounds shrimp, peeled
6 heaping cooking spoons Tony Chachere's seasoning	Tony Chachere's seasoning, to taste
6 heaping cooking spoons salt	¼ cup green onions, chopped
4 bunches green onions, chopped	

1. Make a medium to dark roux with vegetable oil and flour.
2. Add onions and cook for 10 to 15 minutes.
3. Add celery and bell pepper and cook additional 10 to 15 minutes.
4. Slowly add stock (if making "fair size" stew, use water and 1 pound of finely chopped shrimp instead of stock), taking time to incorporate all liquid before adding additional liquid.
5. Cook mixture for 30 minutes to 1 hour at a simmer before adding shrimp.
6. Cook shrimp for 30 minutes adding Tony Chachere's seasoning (additional seasoning if making "fair size") and green onions in last 10 minutes.

Walt Lanier

SUMMER

Summer in Thibodaux is simply put, hot. As a result, we tend to flock to water, in whatever form. Lakes, bayous, beaches and pools are where you will find most residents, likely enjoying lots of delicious food on long summer days. Fresh local seafood abounds —shrimp, crabs, speckled trout, red fish, red snapper, flounder, tuna, bass and catfish fill summer menus. The warm weather also brings with it bountiful summer gardens bursting with gorgeous produce.

IN SEASON

AVOCADOS	EGGPLANT	BANANA PEPPERS
BELL PEPPERS	FIGS	SQUASH
BLACKBERRIES	GREEN TOMATOES	TOMATILLOS
BLUEBERRIES	JALAPENOS	TOMATOES
CANTALOUPE	OKRA	WATERMELON
CUCUMBERS	PEACHES	ZUCCHINI
	PINEAPPLES	

SUMMER STARTERS

REMOULADE SAUCE

Serves: 5 to 6 cups

Refrigerate leftovers and enjoy all week as a dipping sauce or dressing.

4 cups mayonnaise

¾ cup hot mustard

3 ounces lemon juice

¼ cup capers, finely chopped

4 cloves garlic, finely chopped

¼ cup parsley, finely chopped

¼ cup green onions, finely chopped

1 ½ tablespoons dry mustard

2 tablespoons fresh dill, chopped

dash of red pepper

1. Whisk all ingredients together.
2. Serve with shrimp or a salad.

David Jones,
former Envie Restaurant

TUNA POKE

Unique way to eat fresh tuna.

2 green onions, diced

juice of ½ a lime or lemon

1 teaspoon fresh ginger, grated

¼ cup low sodium soy sauce

1 tablespoon rice wine vinegar

1 tablespoon ponzu sauce

¾ teaspoon sesame oil

¼ teaspoon sea salt

¼ teaspoon pepper

1 tablespoon thick soy sauce (optional)

¼ to ½ teaspoon chili paste (optional)

1 pound fresh sashimi tuna, properly handled, cut into ½ inch cubes

1 avocado, cut into ½ inch cubes

fried wonton wrappers or crackers

1. Whisk together green onions, citrus juice, ginger, soy sauce, rice wine vinegar, ponzu, sesame oil, salt, pepper, thick soy sauce and chili paste.

2. Toss mixture with tuna and avocado.

3. Keep cold. If kept in refrigerator, acid from citrus juice will ceviche fish, which may cause a color change in the tuna.

4. Serve with flash fried wonton wrappers or crackers.

Christopher and Anne Rodrigue

FRIED GREEN TOMATOES

Serves: 10 to 14

1 quart buttermilk

2 to 3 cloves garlic, split

2 ½ tablespoons basil, sliced and
tightly packed

1 tablespoon green Tabasco sauce

5 green tomatoes, cut into ½ inch
thick slices

salt, to taste

fish fry

vegetable oil

1. To make marinade, mix buttermilk, garlic, basil and Tabasco sauce in a large bowl.

2. Marinate sliced green tomatoes in mixture for a minimum of 2 hours.

3. Without draining off excess buttermilk, remove tomatoes and season both sides with salt.

4. Dredge tomatoes in fish fry, adding additional salt to each side of the tomato if desired.

5. Carefully fry slices in sauté pan with heated vegetable oil over medium high.

6. Lightly brown one side, then flip over and brown the other side, 2 to 4 minutes per side.

7. Drain on paper towels and serve hot.

8. The inside of the tomatoes should be soft and the crust should be crunchy.

Chef Jean-Paul Bourgeois

CHEF
JEAN-PAUL BOURGEOIS

HOMETOWN:

Houma, Louisiana

EDUCATION AND EXPERIENCE:

Chef Jean-Paul earned a Bachelor of Science Degree in Culinary Arts from the Chef John Folse Culinary Institute at Nicholls State University. After graduation, Chef Jean-Paul worked as a Sous Chef, Chef de Cuisine and Executive Chef in France, California, Atlanta, St. Thomas USVI and New York. Most recently, he served as the Executive Chef at Blue Smoke in New York City. He is currently writing for print and digital publications and has a personal culinary label, Jean-Paul Bourgeois.

"I still dearly miss the outdoors, hunting and fishing. I am passionate about talking about southern food and its place in American cuisine."

BLACKBERRY BAKED BRIE

Serves: 10

You can prepare brie in the puff pastry in advance and store in refrigerator until ready to bake. Try with different fillings such as peach or blueberry preserves, strawberry jam and balsamic vinegar or pesto, sun-dried tomatoes and pine nuts.

1 puff pastry sheet, defrosted

8 ounce round Brie cheese

5 tablespoons seedless blackberry jam, divided

1 egg

1 tablespoon water

2 tablespoons honey

4 tablespoons roasted or candied walnut pieces

fresh blackberries, to garnish

1. Preheat oven to 400 degrees.
2. Lightly flour working surface and roll out puff pastry sheet.
3. Place Brie round in center of the sheet and top with 3 tablespoons of blackberry jam.
4. Wrap Brie with puff pastry sheet and secure edges by pinching them closed.
5. Place Brie on greased or parchment paper lined baking sheet.
6. Lightly beat egg and water and brush over puff pastry.
7. Bake for 20 to 25 minutes until the puff pastry is golden brown.
8. Remove from oven and allow to cool.
9. Stir together remaining jam and honey in a small bowl and drizzle the mixture over the top of the puff pastry.
10. Sprinkle with walnuts and garnish with fresh blackberries.
11. Serve immediately with crackers or crusty bread.

Courtney Lichenstein

FRUIT SALSA AND CINNAMON CHIPS

Serves: 6 to 8

For an impressive presentation, serve in a hollowed out pineapple.

SALSA

1 cup strawberries, finely chopped

1 (15 ounce) can mandarin oranges, chopped

3 kiwi, peeled and finely chopped

1 (8 ounce) can unsweetened crushed pineapple, drained

1 tablespoon lemon juice

1 teaspoon sugar

CINNAMON CHIPS

10 (8 inch) flour tortillas

¼ cup butter, melted

¼ cup sugar

1 teaspoon ground cinnamon

1. Preheat oven to 325 degrees.
2. Combine strawberries, oranges, kiwi, pineapple, lemon juice and sugar in a bowl and refrigerate until ready to serve.
3. Once set, drain excessive juice before serving.
4. For chips, brush tortillas with butter and cut into 8 wedges.
5. Combine sugar and cinnamon and sprinkle over tortillas.
6. Place on ungreased baking sheet.
7. Bake for 10 minutes or until crisp.
8. Serve with fruit salsa.

Cheri Wood

BLACK BEAN SALSA

Serves: 6 to 8

Serve salsa with tortilla chips, to accompany grilled chicken breast or to dress up a simple green salad. Best when made 1 to 2 hours ahead of time and allowed to chill.

2 (15.25 ounce) cans black beans, drained and rinsed

1 (15.25 ounce) can corn, drained

4 green onions, chopped

1 red onion, chopped

2 Roma tomatoes, seeded and chopped

1 bunch cilantro, stems removed and chopped

juice of 2 limes

2 teaspoons cumin

2 tablespoons vegetable oil

salt and pepper, to taste

1. Combine all ingredients and stir.
2. Season with salt and pepper.

Anne Rodrigue

MIK'S SALSA

Serves: 6 to 8

1 (28 ounce) can tomatoes

1 tablespoon garlic powder

1 to 2 jalapeno(s), seeded, to desired heat

½ bunch cilantro, stems removed

juice from 2 limes

1 tablespoon salt

1. Blend all ingredients in a food processor.
2. Serve with chips.

Kristi Ellender

POLLY'S STUFFED JALAPENO PEPPERS

Serves: 10 to 12

30 large fresh jalapeno peppers,
   cut in half length ways and seeded

2 pounds of breakfast sausage
   (recommend hot Jimmy Dean)

16 ounces Velveeta cheese, cubed

12 ounces crabmeat

1 to 2 cup(s) Italian breadcrumbs

1. Preheat oven to 400 degrees.
2. Blanch peppers for 2 to 5 minutes in boiling water.
3. Boil longer for a milder flavor.
4. Drain the peppers and cool.
5. Brown sausage in a skillet and drain grease.
6. Add cheese and stir constantly until melted.
7. Remove from heat and fold in crabmeat.
8. Stir in breadcrumbs until the consistency is thick enough to hold shape.
9. Stuff the pepper halves with mixture and place on a baking sheet.
10. Dust with breadcrumbs.
11. Bake until golden brown, approximately 20 minutes.

B J Rodrigue

CRAB STACK

Serves: 2 to 4

For a Cajun variation, eliminate the mangoes, substitute green onions for red onions, substitute parsley for cilantro and use the same dressing or seafood sauce.

DRESSING

1 to 2 tablespoon(s) cilantro, chopped

½ cup lime juice

2 teaspoons orange juice

¼ teaspoon garlic powder

½ cup olive oil (recommend extra light)

½ teaspoon powdered sugar

salt and pepper, to taste

STACK

½ pound lump crab meat

2 avocados, chopped

2 tomatoes, seeded and chopped

2 mangoes, chopped

1 tablespoon red onion, chopped

1. Combine all ingredients for the dressing and set aside until ready to serve.

2. To make the crab stack, use a clean empty can or a ring mold, alternate stacking ingredients (except red onion).

3. Can make as many layers as desired.

4. Push down after each layer to form a firm stack.

5. Pull up the can/mold to reveal a beautiful stack.

6. Top with extra crab meat, red onion and cilantro.

7. Pour dressing over stack when ready to serve.

8. May serve with crackers.

Jerrie Tyler

CRABMEAT AIOLI DIP

Serves: 4 to 6

½ cup buttermilk

1/3 cup mayonnaise

2 teaspoons Hidden Valley ranch dressing seasoning mix

1 tablespoon Zatarain's creole mustard

1 pound fresh Louisiana jumbo lump crabmeat

1. Combine buttermilk, mayonnaise, ranch seasoning mix and mustard until well blended.
2. Fold in crabmeat being careful not to break the meat apart.
3. Serve with crackers.

Jeanne Peltier Chiasson

CLASSIC HUMMUS

Serves: 4 to 6

Best when chilled for a few hours before serving.

2 cloves garlic

1 teaspoon salt

1 can chickpeas, drained

3 tablespoons tahini

¼ cup water

¼ cup lemon juice

paprika, to garnish

1. In food processor, blend garlic and salt.
2. Add chickpeas and blend.
3. Add tahini, water and lemon juice and blend on high until you get a smooth texture, approximately 2 to 3 minutes.
4. Taste and add more lemon juice and salt if needed.
5. Gradually add more water to preferred consistency.
6. Sprinkle paprika on top before serving.
7. Serve with pita chips or fresh vegetables.

Marcie Elias

MOSCOW MULE

Serves: 1 drink

cold copper mug

juice from ½ lime

2 shots vodka (recommend
   Tito's Vodka)

2 big splashes Sprite

¾ to 1 bottle ginger beer (recommend
   Reed's Jamaican Ginger Beer)

2 to 3 fresh mint leaves

1. Mix all ingredients, except the mint, in a cold
   copper mug.

2. Slap the mint leaves individually between your hands to
   release the aroma.

3. Add mint leaves to the drink and fill the mug with ice.

David Elias

FRONT PORCH SWING

Light and refreshing summer cocktail.

3 cucumber slices

1 ounce Pimm's liquor

2 ounces gin

½ ounce lemon juice

½ ounce simple syrup

1 bottle ginger beer

1 cucumber spear or slices, to garnish

1. Muddle cucumber slices in a glass.
2. Add Pimm's, gin, lemon juice and simple syrup.
3. Top with ice.
4. Add ginger beer and mix.
5. Garnish with cucumber.

Kimberly Neal

COSMOPOLITANS

Serves: 2 to 3 drinks

*This recipe was perfected by good friends in Grand Isle, Louisiana.
It's perfect for warm summer nights.*

½ cup vodka

¼ cup triple sec

1 cup cranberry or pomegranate/
cranberry juice

¼ cup lime juice

lime slices, to garnish

1. Mix all liquid ingredients in shaker with ice.

2. Pour into martini glasses.

3. Garnish with lime slices.

Brenda Riviere and Penny Weimer

LEGACY COOLER REDUX

Serves: 20 to 25

An updated version of our original "Legacy" Cooler (PMS 169 Punch).

2 (6 ounce) cans frozen lemonade concentrate, thawed and undiluted

16 ounces Looza Peach Nectar

4 ounces fresh lime juice

1 cup St. Germaine Elderflower liqueur

1 cup vodka (optional)

3 bottles dry sparkling rosé wine, chilled

3 lemons, sliced

3 limes, sliced

1. In a gallon size pitcher or punch bowl combine lemonade concentrate, nectar, lime juice, St. Germain and vodka. Chill well.

2. Just before serving, slowly add chilled sparkling rosé.

3. Pour over ice and garnish with lemon and lime slices.

4. To maintain the sparkle over a longer period of time, mix all ingredients except rosé. When serving, add 5 ounces of rosé to 3 ounces of mix.

Jeffery Markel

WATERMELON SALAD

Serves: 6

Can substitute feta cheese for Cheddar cheese.

LIME VINAIGRETTE

5 tablespoons fresh lime juice

½ teaspoon lime zest

1 tablespoon dark brown sugar

½ teaspoon kosher salt

½ teaspoon ground black pepper

5 tablespoons extra virgin olive oil

SALAD

8 cups watermelon, cubed

1 cup Cheddar cheese, cubed

¾ cup pecans, raw or lightly roasted

1. To make vinaigrette, combine lime juice, zest, sugar, salt and pepper in bowl, blend well.

2. Drizzle in the oil slowly while whisking, creating an emulsion.

3. In a Ziploc bag, marinate watermelon with vinaigrette for approximately 30 minutes.

4. Toss Cheddar cheese and pecans with watermelon and serve.

5. Can be served over greens.

Chef Jean-Paul Bourgeois

LOUISIANA CRAB AND BRIE SOUP

Serves: 8 to 10

Soup is so rich it can also be used to top fish, chicken or a steak.

CRAB STOCK

2 pounds fresh Louisiana blue
  crabs, boiled

4 tablespoons olive oil

1 yellow onion, diced

1 carrot, diced

3 ribs celery, diced

1 clove garlic, minced

2 bay leaves

2 ounces brandy

1 cup white wine

2 quarts of water

SOUP

½ cup unsalted butter

¾ cup flour

1 quart crab stock

1 ½ quarts heavy whipping cream

8 ounces Brie cheese

1 teaspoon salt

1 teaspoon white pepper

1 teaspoon cayenne pepper

1 pound jumbo Louisiana
  lump crabmeat

1. To make the crab stock, crack open crabs with a meat mallet or hammer until meat is exposed.

2. Break legs, claws and body cavity into pieces about 1 inch in size.

3. In a 1 gallon stockpot, heat olive oil; add cracked crabs and sauté for 5 minutes.

4. Add onion, carrot, celery, garlic and bay leaves; continue to sauté for 5 minutes.

5. Add brandy, white wine and water; bring to a simmer over medium heat and cook for 45 minutes.

6. The liquid should just cover the crab shells as stock cooks, if it doesn't, add a little more water.

7. Cool, then strain stock through a fine-mesh strainer several times to remove crab pieces.

8. Set aside. You should have approximately 1 quart of stock.

9. In a soup pot, melt butter and blend in flour until smooth and creamy; simmer over low heat for 1 minute.

10. Slowly add crab stock mixture using a wire whisk to blend until roux is dissolved.

11. Add heavy cream and simmer for 10 minutes.

12. Remove outside rind from Brie cheese and discard.

13. Cut cheese into 1 inch cubes and add to stock stirring constantly until cheese completely melts.

14. Season soup with salt, white pepper and cayenne.

15. Add jumbo lump crabmeat and serve.

Vance and Dee Dee Broussard
(adopted from Dakota Restaurant)

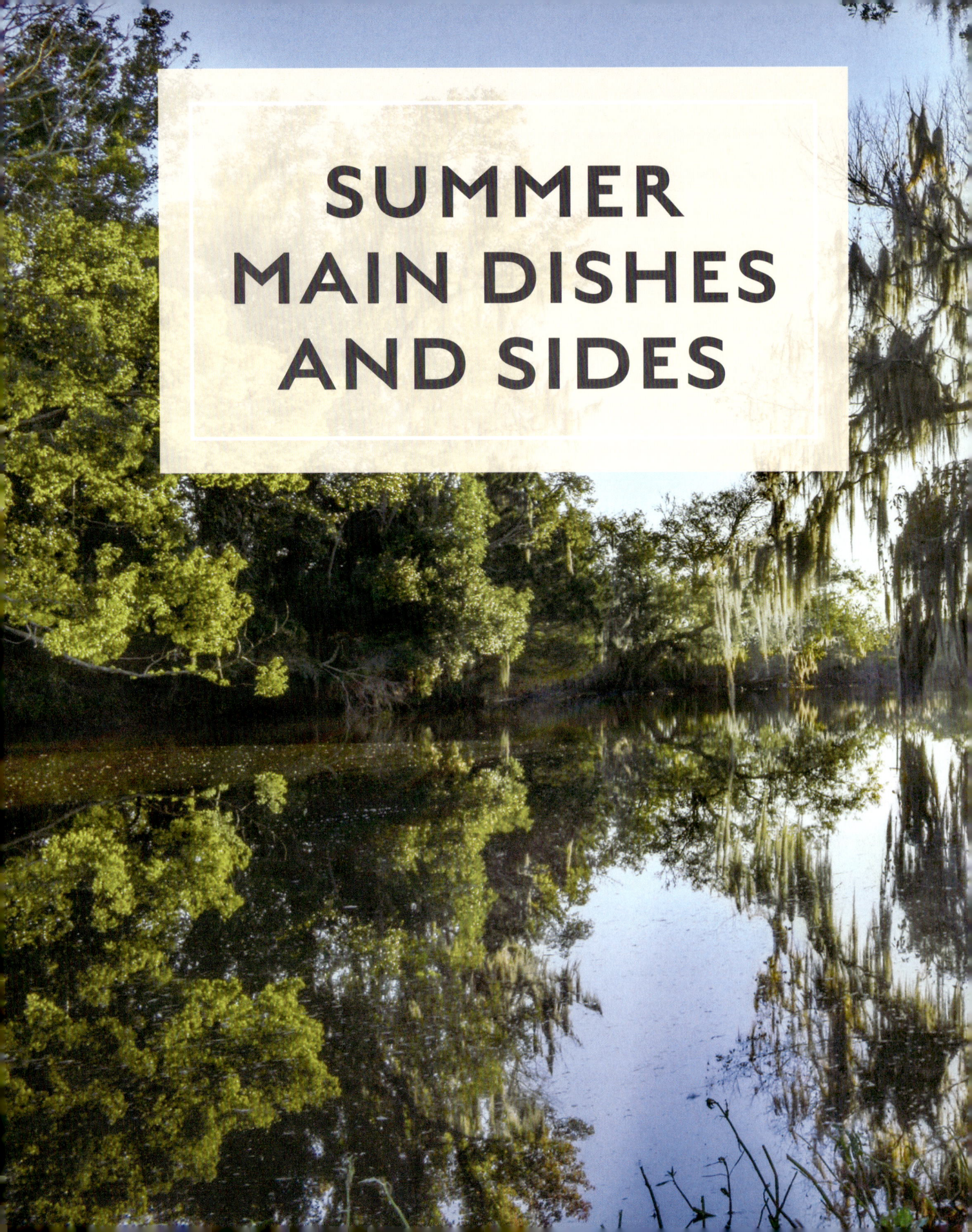

SUMMER
MAIN DISHES
AND SIDES

BLANCHARD'S SEAFOOD BOIL

This is an easy stove top boil recipe for a small crowd.

1 gallon water

12 medium sized live crabs or 4 to 5
   pounds raw shrimp, heads on

1 yellow onion, whole

1 to 2 tablespoon(s) Zatarain's Liquid
   Crab Boil

6 to 8 red potatoes (optional)

5 tablespoons salt (more if potatoes
   are not used)

1 tablespoon mustard (only if using crabs)

2 to 3 cloves garlic

1 lemon, halved

1. Put all ingredients except ½ of the lemon into a large stove top boiling pot.

2. Bring to a full boil.

3. Continue boiling as follows: for crabs, 20 minutes; for small shrimp, 5 minutes; medium shrimp, 10 minutes; large shrimp, 15 minutes.

4. Remove from heat.

5. Add remaining lemon half.

6. Allow to soak 10 to 20 minutes.

7. Drain through a colander or wire basket, then dump on the table and enjoy.

1982 Louisiana Legacy Cookbook

FRIED SOFT SHELL CRAB
WITH CRABMEAT SAUCE

Serves: 6

Garnish with parsley and/or green onions, if desired.

SOFT SHELL CRAB

2 eggs, beaten

2 tablespoons mustard

1 can evaporated milk

1 teaspoon plus 1 tablespoon Tony Chachere's seasoning

1 ½ cups instant mashed potatoes

1 ½ cups corn flour

6 large soft shell crabs, cleaned

peanut oil, for frying

SAUCE

½ cup butter

2 medium white onions, chopped

1 (14.75 ounce) can creamed style sweet corn

1 (10.5 ounce) can cream of mushroom soup

1 pint heavy whipping cream

1 pound jumbo lump crab meat

1 cap liquid crab boil

pinch of salt

evaporated milk

1. Mix eggs, mustard and evaporated milk to make a wash for the crab.
2. Add 1 teaspoon Tony Chachere's seasoning to the wash and mix well.
3. In a separate bowl mix the instant potatoes and corn flour with 1 tablespoon Tony Chachere's seasoning, more to taste.
4. Dip crabs in liquid mixture then roll in flour potato mixture and deep fry in peanut oil.
5. In a medium sized sauce pan melt butter and onions, sauté until clear.
6. Add creamed corn and sauté for a few minutes until hot.
7. Do not cook on high heat, sauce is best made slowly.
8. Add cream of mushroom soup and cook down for 5 to 10 minutes.
9. Add whipping cream.
10. Cook for several minutes until well combined and hot throughout.
11. Add ½ of crab meat to sauce, season with liquid crab boil and salt.
12. Use the evaporated milk to thin gravy to desired consistency.
13. If too thin cook for a few more minutes until sauce thickens.
14. Place fried crab on serving dish, shell on bottom and add a large serving spoon of sauce over soft shell crab.
15. Top with remaining crab meat.

Craig Perque

BAYOU FISH FRY

Serves: 4

1 pound fish fillets

salt and pepper, to taste

season-all, to taste

½ cup yellow mustard

frying oil

2 cups fish fry

cornmeal (optional)

1. Season fish with salt, pepper and season-all.
2. Spread with mustard and set aside.
3. In a fryer, heat enough oil to deep fry.
4. Place fish fry or a mixture of half fish fry and half cornmeal in a small paper bag.
5. Place a few fillets in the bag and shake to coat well.
6. Remove from bag and place in hot oil.
7. Fry until golden brown and crispy.
8. When done, drain on absorbent paper towels and serve immediately.

1982 Louisiana Legacy Cookbook

BEER BATTER SHRIMP

Serves: 4

1 egg, beaten

½ teaspoon Worcestershire sauce

½ teaspoon Louisiana Hot Sauce

2 ounces beer

1 pound large shrimp, peeled, deveined and fantailed

1 ½ cups all-purpose flour, divided

salt and pepper, to taste

¾ inch frying oil

1. Combine egg, Worcestershire sauce, Louisiana Hot Sauce and beer in a bowl.
2. Add shrimp and mix.
3. Add ½ cup flour and stir.
4. In a separate bowl, combine 1 cup flour with salt and pepper.
5. Dip shrimp, 1 at a time, in flour and fry in hot cooking oil in a heavy skillet until golden brown, turning shrimp to brown evenly.
6. When done, drain on absorbent paper towels and serve immediately.

1982 Louisiana Legacy Cookbook

TARTAR SAUCE

Serves: 1 cup

¾ cup mayonnaise

3 tablespoons sweet pickle, chopped

2 tablespoons olives or capers,
 finely chopped

1 tablespoon parsley, finely chopped

1 tablespoon chives or onions,
 finely chopped

1 teaspoon horseradish

1. Combine all ingredients; blend well.
2. Serve with fried fish or shellfish.

Barbara Mendoza

FISH TACOS

Serves: 4 to 6

MANGO SALSA

1 cup mango, peeled and chopped

1 cup tomato, chopped

¼ cup red onion, diced

3 tablespoons cilantro, chopped

2 teaspoons lime juice

salt and pepper, to taste

TACOS

2 pounds fresh white flaky fish fillets (trout, red snapper, etc.)

salt and pepper, to taste (or other desired seasoning such as chili powder, cumin, paprika)

8 (8 inch) corn tortillas

2 avocados, chopped

1 cup mixed greens (optional)

sour cream, to garnish

green onions, to garnish

1. To make the mango salsa, add all ingredients together in a small bowl and toss.

2. Set aside.

3. Season the fish evenly with salt and pepper or other desired seasoning.

4. In a nonstick pan over medium high heat, cook the seasoned fish for approximately 5 minutes on each side or until fish cooked through and flaky.

5. Set fish aside and heat the tortillas in the pan, 1 at a time for approximately 1 minute on each side.

6. Assemble tacos with fish evenly divided.

7. Top tacos with avocados, mixed greens and desired amount of mango salsa.

8. Garnish with sour cream and green onions.

9. Serve immediately.

Heather Howard

GRILLED SNAPPER

Serves: 4

Grilled fish with a kick.

¼ cup green olives, pitted and chopped

2 tablespoons capers

1 pint cherry tomatoes

1 handful fresh parsley, roughly chopped

juice of 1 lime

¼ cup olive oil

1 jalapeno, chopped

4 fillets fresh snapper

Tony Chachere's seasoning, to taste

garlic powder, to taste

onion powder, to taste

1. Heat the grill to medium low.

2. In a mixing bowl, combine olives, capers, cherry tomatoes, parsley, lime juice, olive oil and jalapeno.

3. To assemble the grilling packets, fold 4 sheets of aluminum foil in half lengthwise and then unfold and lay them on the counter.

4. Season each fillet lightly with Tony Chachere's, garlic powder and onion powder and place it on 1 side of the foil, parallel to the crease.

5. Top each fillet with ¼ of the salsa mixture.

6. Fold the foil over so it covers the fish completely and then roll the edges tightly to seal the package.

7. Place the packets on the grill grate and close the lid.

8. With the lid down, the grill temperature should max out around 450 degrees.

9. Cook the fillets until they're cooked all the way through, approximately 8 to 10 minutes.

Brad "Beaver" Hymel

JUNICE'S SAUCY FISH

Serves: 4 to 6

Perfect to make at the camp because ingredients are common pantry staples.

1 onion, sliced

1 teaspoon olive oil

1 tablespoon ketchup

1 ½ tablespoons mayonnaise

1 tablespoon Worcestershire sauce

4 tablespoons butter, melted

1 tablespoon mustard

1 tablespoon red wine vinegar

¼ cup Italian dressing

fresh fish fillets to cover bottom of pan

salt and pepper, to taste

paprika, to taste

1 (4 ounce) can mushrooms

1. Preheat oven to 350 degrees.
2. Sauté onion in olive oil and set aside.
3. In container, mix ketchup, mayonnaise, Worcestershire sauce, butter, mustard, red wine vinegar and Italian dressing.
4. Season fish to taste with salt, pepper and paprika.
5. Line buttered 9 x 13 inch pan with seasoned fish fillets.
6. Top fish with sautéed onions, mushrooms and sauce mixture.
7. Bake for 30 to 40 minutes.
8. Serve with garlic bread to dip.

Robbie Naquin

POTATO CHIP CRUSTED REDFISH

Serves: 6

Try this recipe with any fresh Gulf fish.

3 tablespoons vegetable oil

6 (5 ounce) redfish fillets,
   rinsed and deboned

Cajun seasoning, to taste

2 cups white flour

2 eggs

2 cups milk

10 ounces Zapp's Cajun Crawtator chips,
   crushed into small pieces

Louisiana Crab and Corn Relish
   (recipe below)

1. Heat oil in skillet over low to medium heat.
2. Season redfish with Cajun seasoning.
3. Coat fish with white flour.
4. Combine eggs and milk to make egg wash.
5. Dip fish in egg wash.
6. Coat fish with crushed chips.
7. Pan fry fish on both sides for 4 to 5 minutes or until done.
8. Top with a spoonful of Louisiana Crab and Corn Relish.

LOUISIANA CRAB AND CORN RELISH

Serves: 6

2 tablespoons olive oil

2 ears fresh corn, cut off the cob

1 tablespoon garlic, minced

½ cup red onion, diced

½ cup green bell pepper, diced

¼ cup red wine vinegar

1 cup creole tomatoes, diced

2 tablespoons parsley, chopped

salt and pepper, to taste

½ pound fresh Louisiana
   jumbo lump crabmeat

1. Heat olive oil in skillet.
2. Sauté corn in skillet for approximately 3 minutes.
3. Add garlic and sauté for 1 additional minute.
4. Remove from heat.
5. Add onion and bell pepper to skillet and toss.
6. Put sautéed vegetable mix into bowl.
7. Mix in vinegar, tomatoes and parsley.
8. Season with salt and pepper to taste.
9. Fold in crabmeat.

Chef Kevin Templet

CHEF KEVIN TEMPLET

HOMETOWN:

Labadieville, Louisiana

EDUCATION AND EXPERIENCE:
Chef Kevin learned to cook through research and practice on his own and through competing in 4-H cooking competitions. He worked at Uncle's Grocery Store and Meat Market, Western Sizzlin, Flanagan's Creative Food and Drink and is now the Executive Chef at Fremin's in Thibodaux.

"One of the many things I love about Thibodaux is the wonderful small town and community vibe we have here. I also love that we are surrounded by such beautiful nature and water that is so plentiful with its seafood bounty. Fishing and spending time on the water is one of my favorite things."

REDFISH COURTBOUILLON

Serves: 6

A labor of love.

FISH STOCK

1 (6 to 7 pound) redfish, filleted and
 deboned (reserve bones to make stock)

1 quart water

onions, to taste

celery, to taste

carrots, to taste

bay leaves, to taste

other desired seasonings

COURTBOUILLON

¼ cup parsley, chopped

1 tablespoon Worcestershire sauce

3 ounces dry red wine

1 cup flour

1 cup oil

2 onions, finely chopped

1 (6 ounce) can tomato paste

½ teaspoon sugar

1 (10 ounce) can whole tomatoes

4 cloves garlic, minced

2 slices lemon

4 whole cloves

4 bay leaves

1 tablespoon basil

3 stalks celery, finely chopped

1 bell pepper, finely chopped

½ cup green onion tops, finely chopped

fish stock

1 (8 ounce) can mushrooms, drained
 or fresh mushrooms

salt and pepper, to taste

cooked rice

1. Make a fish stock by simmering the fish bones in enough water to cover (at least 1 quart) adding seasonings (onions, celery, carrots, bay leaves, etc.) to your liking.

2. Simmer for approximately 30 to 40 minutes.

3. Strain stock a few times and set aside.

4. Marinate the parsley in Worcestershire sauce and wine, set aside.

5. In a black iron pot or heavy saucepan, combine flour with hot oil.

6. Stir constantly over low heat until a dark brown roux is formed.

7. Add onions and cook approximately 10 minutes, stirring often.

8. Add tomato paste and sugar, cooking at least 10 minutes or until loose in the pot.

9. Add whole tomatoes and garlic. Cook 10 minutes more.

10. Stud lemon slices with whole cloves, then add lemon, bay leaves and basil followed by celery, bell pepper and green onions, sautéing after each vegetable is added.

11. Add fish stock to thin gravy to desired consistency. It should be relatively thick and rich.

12. Cook for 30 minutes on low heat, stirring often. The gravy can be prepared to this point and frozen. When needed just defrost add fish and parsley marinade.

13. Add fish fillets, cut into serving size pieces, simmer for 10 minutes, stirring carefully so as not to break up fish.

14. Add parsley marinade and mushrooms and cook for 5 minutes more, mixing carefully.

15. Remove from heat, cover and let stand for 10 to 15 minutes.

16. Remove bay leaves and lemons. Season with salt and pepper to taste.

17. Serve over rice.

Ridley Gros

SHRIMP FETTUCCINI

Serves: 4 to 6

Packed with Louisiana heat. For a less spicy version, use regular Velveeta cheese.

16 ounces Cajun vegetable trinity

2 cloves garlic, chopped

1 ½ sticks butter

2 teaspoons salt

½ teaspoon cayenne pepper

½ teaspoon black pepper

3 pounds fresh shrimp, peeled
and deveined

1 tablespoon flour

8 ounces Jalapeno Velveeta cheese, cubed

1 cup half and half cream

8 ounces fettuccini noodles, cooked

1 tablespoon parsley flakes, to garnish

1. Preheat oven to 300 degrees.
2. Sauté vegetable trinity and garlic in butter until softened.
3. Add salt, cayenne and black pepper.
4. Add shrimp and sauté.
5. Add flour, cheese and half and half and cook until cheese is melted.
6. Mix in cooked drained noodles.
7. Pour in 9 x 13 inch buttered dish and bake 15 minutes.
8. Garnish with parsley flakes.

Barbara Moore

LEILA'S EGGPLANT, SHRIMP AND CRABMEAT CASSEROLE

Serves: 4 to 8

When this recipe was tested for the 1982 publication of the Louisiana Legacy cookbook, it was rated as a "four star" favorite. The same is true today. You will not be disappointed with this local favorite.

2 medium eggplants, peeled and diced

1 to 2 cup(s) water

½ cup butter

1 cup onions, chopped

¼ cup celery, chopped

¼ cup green pepper, chopped

1 clove garlic, minced

1 slice bread, moistened

1 cup seasoned breadcrumbs

1 cup raw shrimp, peeled and drained

1 cup white crab meat, drained

1. Cook eggplant, for approximately 5 to 10 minutes, in a medium sized saucepan in enough water to cover.

2. While this is cooking, melt butter in another saucepan.

3. Add onions, celery, green pepper and garlic; cook until soft.

4. Drain eggplant, mash and add to vegetable seasonings.

5. Stir in bread and ½ cup of seasoned breadcrumbs.

6. Cook approximately 5 minutes, mixing well.

7. Fold in raw shrimp and crabmeat and cook on medium heat until shrimp are done, approximately 10 minutes.

8. Stir often so that shrimp cook evenly.

9. Spoon into a 1 ½ quart casserole dish or individual ramekins, top with remaining breadcrumbs and dot with butter.

10. Place under broiler a few minutes to brown.

1982 Louisiana Legacy Cookbook

SHRIMP AND GRITS

Serves: 6

Enjoy leftover grits for breakfast the next day.

GRITS

2 cups chicken broth

1 cup heavy whipping cream

2 cups water

1 ¼ cup quick cooking grits

pinch of salt

2 tablespoons butter

½ cup Parmesan cheese, shredded

salt, to taste

white pepper, to taste

SHRIMP

2 tablespoons olive oil

1 yellow onion, diced

1 green bell pepper, diced

1 jalapeno pepper, seeded and diced

2 links of Cajun smoked sausage, sliced into half moons

1 pound shrimp (40 to 50 count), peeled and deveined

1 (14.5 ounce) can petite diced tomatoes

2 tablespoons Worcestershire sauce

salt and pepper, to taste

cayenne pepper, to taste

1. To make grits, in a heavy-bottomed saucepan, bring chicken broth, whipping cream and water to a low simmer.

2. While simmering, whisk in the grits and a pinch of salt, returning to a low simmer.

3. Cook until thickened, stirring often, approximately 5 minutes.

4. Stir in butter and Parmesan cheese.

5. Season to taste with salt and white pepper.

6. Heat a large sauté pan over medium heat.

7. Add olive oil and sauté onion, bell pepper and jalapeno until tender.

8. Add sausage and cook uncovered an additional 10 minutes.

9. When the sausage is cooked, add shrimp, can of diced tomatoes and Worcestershire sauce

10. Cook covered for 15 minutes.

11. Season with salt, black pepper and cayenne pepper to taste.

12. Serve over warm grits.

Josh Becnel

SHRIMP AND SPAGHETTI ETOUFFEE

Serves: 6 to 8

This recipe substitutes noodles for rice as a variation of "etouffee."

2 large onions, chopped

1/3 cup olive oil

½ cup water

1 sweet pepper, chopped

1 (12 ounce) package smoked
    sausage, sliced

2 (8 ounce) cans tomato sauce

1 (6 ounce) can tomato paste

2 teaspoons sugar

1 ½ pounds raw shrimp, peeled

1 quart hot water

1 pound thin spaghetti, uncooked

4 tablespoons butter

salt and pepper, to taste

1. Sauté onions in oil until lightly brown.
2. Add ½ cup water, sweet pepper and sausage.
3. Cook for 20 minutes on low heat.
4. Add tomato sauce, tomato paste and sugar.
5. Simmer for 1 ½ hours.
6. Add shrimp and cook for 25 minutes.
7. Add 1 quart hot water and bring to a boil.
8. Add spaghetti, stirring often.
9. Cook on low heat until spaghetti noodles are tender.
10. Add additional hot water as needed.
11. Remove from heat.
12. Stir in butter and season with salt and pepper to taste.

Therese Dobard

QUINOA STUFFED BELL PEPPERS

Serves: 8

BAKED CHICKEN AND CHICKEN STOCK

1 small whole chicken

salt, to taste

black pepper, to taste

granulated garlic, to taste

red pepper, to taste

1 onion, chopped

2 stalks celery, chopped

2 bay leaves

4 cups water

1 tablespoon corn starch

STUFFED BELL PEPPERS

8 medium bell peppers, tops
  removed and seeded

1 pound ground pork or beef

8 ounces Cajun vegetable trinity

1 cup baked chicken, chopped

1 cup chicken stock

salt and pepper, to taste

Cajun seasoning, to taste

1 cup quinoa, cooked

½ sleeve saltine crackers,
  crushed (optional)

1. Preheat oven to 350 degrees.
2. Season the chicken with salt, black pepper, garlic and red pepper and place in baking pan.
3. Add onion, celery and bay leaves to the pan.
4. Cover and bake for approximately 1 ½ to 2 hours.
5. Debone and chop the chicken and put aside.
6. To make chicken stock, place all leftovers from the chicken pan, including the bones and skin, in approximately 4 cups of water, more if needed to cover the chicken.
7. Boil for approximately 2 hours and strain.
8. Mix corn starch with a small amount of cold water, then add it to the stock.
9. Simmer uncovered until it thickens to a gravy consistency (freeze any extra unused stock).
10. Blanch peppers in boiling water, approximately 3 to 4 minutes, and set aside upside down to drain.
11. Brown ground pork/beef and drain, then add vegetable trinity and sauté.
12. Add chopped chicken and broth and cook for 5 minutes, taste and season with salt, pepper and Cajun seasoning.
13. Remove from heat and stir in the cooked quinoa.
14. Mixture will be wet at this point.
15. Stuff peppers with mixture.
16. Top with crushed crackers if desired.
17. Bake peppers on a baking sheet until heated through and tops are browned, approximately 10 minutes.

BJ Rodrigue

ORZO PASTA SALAD

Serves: 6

Great dish for a shower or to take to a pot luck meal.

VINAIGRETTE DRESSING

¼ cup red wine vinegar

1/3 cup olive oil

2 tablespoons fresh lemon juice

2 teaspoons honey

1 teaspoon sugar

salt and pepper, to taste

PASTA SALAD

12 ounces orzo pasta

6 cups chicken broth

2 cups grape or cherry tomatoes, halved

4 tablespoons green onions, chopped

3 tablespoons fresh basil, chopped

1 cup baby spinach, coarsely chopped

salt and pepper, to taste

garlic salt, to taste

cayenne pepper, to taste

1 cup Feta cheese, crumbled

1. To make dressing, whisk together the vinegar, oil, lemon juice, honey and sugar.

2. Season to taste with a bit of salt and pepper and set aside.

3. For the salad, cook orzo pasta in chicken broth until tender according to package directions.

4. Drain well but do not rinse.

5. Let the pasta cool to room temperature, tossing often so it doesn't stick together.

6. Stir in 1 to 2 tablespoons of the dressing if the pasta is overly sticky.

7. Toss cooled pasta with tomatoes, green onions, basil and spinach.

8. Pour the vinaigrette over the salad and stir to coat all ingredients with the dressing.

9. Season with salt, pepper, garlic salt and cayenne to taste.

10. Add Feta cheese and toss lightly.

11. Serve at room temperature.

Michelle Means

VEGGIE QUINOA

Serves: 2 to 4

3/4 cup quinoa, cooked

1 cup carrots, shredded

1 cup cucumbers, chopped

1 cup snap peas

½ cup golden raisins

¼ cup sunflower seeds

olive oil, to taste

white balsamic vinegar, to taste

salt and pepper, to taste

1. Mix all ingredients together.
2. Drizzle with olive oil and white balsamic vinegar.
3. Add salt and pepper to taste.
4. Serve at room temperature.

Nadine Hebert

PATTI'S TOMATO PIE

Serves: 8 to 16

6 to 8 slices bacon, chopped

½ onion, chopped

2 to 3 creole tomatoes, sliced (can use green tomatoes when creole not in season)

2 Pillsbury pie crusts

2 teaspoons fresh basil, chopped

1 cup fresh Cheddar cheese, grated

1 cup fresh Parmesan cheese, grated

1 cup mayonnaise (add lemon juice to mayonnaise to help spread)

1. Preheat oven to 350 degrees.
2. Sauté bacon and onion until caramelized and drain excess grease.
3. Slice tomatoes, sprinkle with a little salt and drain on paper towels to remove excess moisture.
4. Place bacon and onions on bottom of pie crusts, reserving some bacon for garnish.
5. Place tomato slices on top of bacon and onions.
6. Top with fresh basil, reserving some basil for garnish.
7. Use Cheddar cheese for 1 pie and Parmesan cheese for second pie or combine and sprinkle both cheeses over tomatoes.
8. Spread mayonnaise over cheese to cover top of pie.
9. Bake for 30 to 40 minutes until browned.
10. Garnish with chopped bacon and fresh basil.
11. Let sit at least 15 minutes before slicing.

Jennifer Jones Rodrigue

ZUCCHINI PIE

Serves: 8

A quick and different way to serve summer zucchini.

2 cups fresh summer zucchini, shredded

2 eggs, lightly beaten

1 white onion, chopped

¾ cup Bisquick gluten-free baking mix

¾ cup sharp Cheddar cheese, shredded

½ teaspoon salt

¼ teaspoon black pepper

¼ teaspoon paprika

¼ teaspoon onion powder

shake of garlic powder

1. Preheat oven to 350 degrees.
2. Combine all ingredients and mix well.
3. Transfer to 9 inch greased pie plate.
4. Bake for 45 minutes or until toothpick inserted in center comes out clean.
5. Cool and slice like a pie.

Kimber Ratcliff

CORONATION CHICKEN SALAD

Serves: 8 to 12

Not your traditional chicken salad.

2 tablespoons honey

1 tablespoon curry powder

2 tablespoons white wine or
  white wine vinegar

½ cup Greek yogurt, or to
  desired consistency

½ cup mayonnaise, or to
  desired consistency

2 cooked small chickens,
  deboned and cubed

2 cups red grapes, chopped

½ cup dried apricots, diced

1 cup roasted cashews, chopped

1. In a small saucepan, cook honey and curry powder for approximately 2 minutes.

2. Add wine and cook for 2 more minutes.

3. Let cool.

4. Mix in Greek yogurt and mayonnaise.

5. Fold in all remaining ingredients.

6. Serve on croissants or with crackers.

Shauntelle Sliman Tatford

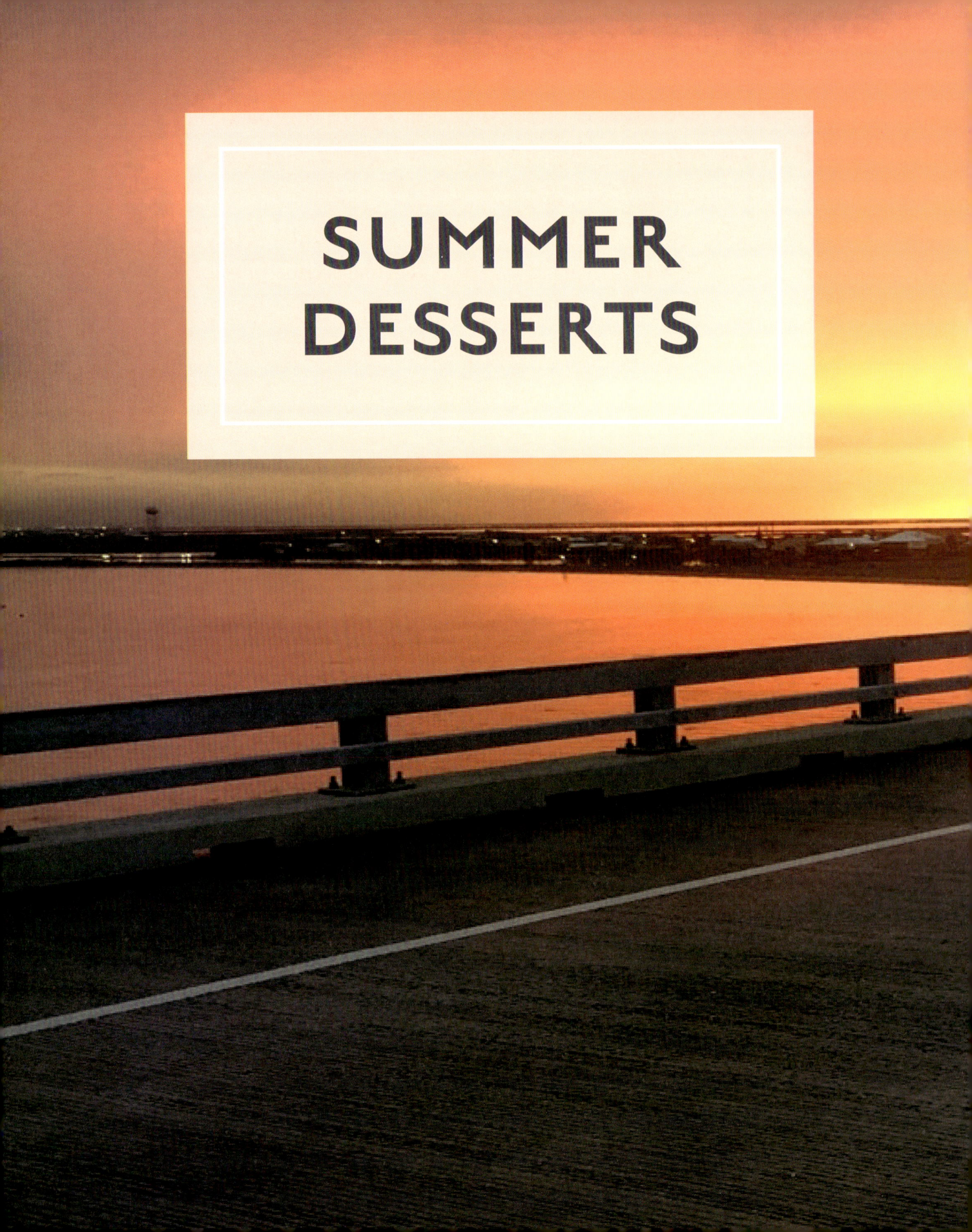

SUMMER DESSERTS

DELIGHTFUL LEMON CAKE

Serves: 12 to 16

CAKE

1 (15.25 ounce) box Duncan Hines yellow cake mix (or lemon cake mix for extra lemon flavor)

1 (3.4 ounce) box instant lemon pudding

¼ cup lemon juice

¾ cup water

¾ cup vegetable oil

3 eggs

GLAZE

2 cups powdered sugar

½ cup lemon juice

1. Preheat oven to 325 degrees.

2. Using a mixer, blend cake mix, lemon pudding mix, lemon juice, water, oil and eggs together for approximately 2 minutes on medium speed, scraping bowl as needed.

3. Spray Bundt pan or 8 ½ x 11 inch cake pan with non-stick spray.

4. Pour batter into greased pan.

5. Bake immediately for 40 minutes or until done.

6. Let cool.

7. Prepare lemon glaze by whisking powdered sugar and lemon juice.

8. Continue to whisk until desired consistency and taste, adding more powdered sugar or lemon juice as desired.

9. Pour glaze on top of cake while cake is still warm in pan.

10. Remove from pan when cooled and sprinkle with sifted powdered sugar.

Sue C Blakeman,
in memory of Helen Marshall

BLACKBERRY DUMPLINGS

Serves: 8 to 10

Freeze leftover blackberry juice and enjoy all year.

BLACKBEARRY JUICE

water

1 gallon freshly picked blackberries

1 ½ cups sugar

DUMPLINGS

2 to 3 cups Bisquick mix

4 tablespoons sugar

1 egg

1 cup milk

fresh blackberries, to garnish

Chelsey Terrebonne Crawford,
Plaisance Family Recipe

1. To make the blackberry juice, add just enough water to cover blackberries and boil until soft.

2. Mash them with a fork or other type of masher and strain blackberry juice into a large pot on medium heat. Should have approximately 4 ½ cups.

3. Add sugar and stir to dissolve.

4. To make dumplings mix together Bisquick, 4 tablespoons sugar, egg and milk.

5. The mixture should be dry.

6. If there is still too much liquid, add more Bisquick (dough is correct when it does not fall off of spoon when turned upside down).

7. Once the blackberry juice has come to a boil, add a small spoonful of dough to the boiling juice 1 at a time, approximately 8 per round.

8. When the edges of the dough look cooked, flip it over in the juice to cook the other side.

9. Once the dough has been cooked through, remove from juice and carefully place dumplings into a large bowl.

10. Continue to add the raw dough mixture into the boiling juice until there is none left, still only adding 8 at a time.

11. Once all of the cooked dumplings have been placed in a large bowl, cover with blackberry juice and garnish with fresh blackberries.

12. Serve warm.

DI'S CHEESECAKE

Serves: 8

This year-round dessert can be topped with fresh seasonal berries in the summer.

CRUST

1 cup graham cracker crumbs

½ cup sugar

2 ½ ounces butter, melted

CHEESECAKE

1 ½ pounds cream cheese, room temperature

1 cup sugar

3 eggs, room temperature

½ tablespoon vanilla extract

1 cup sour cream

½ cup powdered sugar

1. Preheat oven to 325 degrees.

2. To make crust, mix graham cracker crumbs, sugar and butter and pack in a greased 9 inch pie pan.

3. To make cheesecake, beat cream cheese and sugar until there are no lumps.

4. Add eggs, 1 at a time, then add vanilla extract.

5. Pour into the pie crust and bake on the middle rack of the oven for 45 minutes.

6. While baking, in a separate bowl, add sour cream and powdered sugar and mix well.

7. Remove pie from oven and spread a thin layer of sour cream mixture on top of the pie and bake another 15 minutes.

8. The center should be set but not firm.

Carolyn Elias

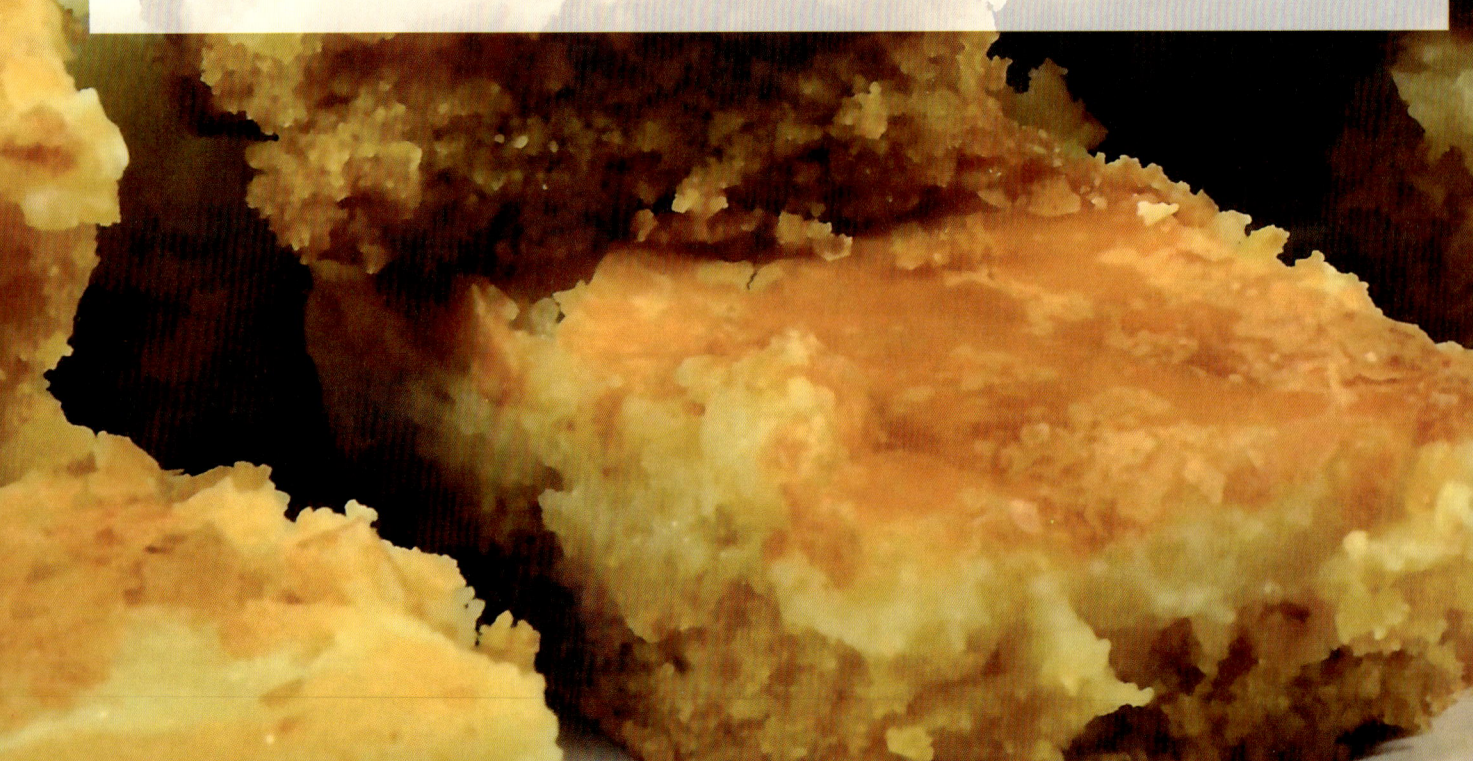

CHESS SQUARES

Serves: 12

3 eggs

1 (16.5 ounce) box yellow cake mix

½ cup butter, softened

1 (16 ounce) box confectioners sugar

8 ounce package cream cheese

1. Preheat oven to 350 degrees.

2. Combine 1 egg, cake mix and softened butter and mix well.

3. Spread mixture in the bottom of a greased 13 x 9 inch pan.

4. Beat together confectioners sugar, cream cheese and 2 eggs.

5. Pour mixture on top of the cake mixture.

6. Bake for 40 to 45 minutes.

Nancy Toups

BANANA SPLIT CAKE

Serves: 10 to 12

A festive 4th of July recipe!

2 cups graham cracker crumbs
(approximately 16 whole crackers)

¼ cup sugar

1 stick butter, melted

1 (8 ounce) package cream cheese, softened

1 teaspoon vanilla extract

2 cups confectioners sugar, sifted

1 (20 ounce) can crushed
pineapple, drained

5 to 6 bananas, sliced

1 (16 ounce) carton Cool Whip

strawberries, to garnish

blueberries, to garnish

1. Mix graham cracker crumbs, sugar and butter together; press into the bottom of a greased 9 x 13 inch pan.

2. Beat cream cheese, vanilla extract and confectioners sugar.

3. Pour over the crust.

4. Pour pineapple on top of the previous layer, then layer the sliced bananas over the pineapple.

5. Spread the Cool Whip over the bananas.

6. Garnish the top with strawberries and blueberries to resemble an American flag.

7. Refrigerate until ready to serve.

Renee B Biondo

PINEAPPLE DREAM CAKE

Serves: 10

1 (15.25 ounce) box yellow cake mix

1 (20 ounce) can crushed
    pineapple, drained

4 ounces cream cheese, room temperature

1 (3.4 ounce) box instant vanilla pudding,
    prepared according to package

Cool Whip

nuts or coconut, to garnish

1. Bake cake as directed.
2. While cake is warm, top with crushed pineapple.
3. Mix together cream cheese and pudding, and put on top of pineapple.
4. Cover with Cool Whip.
5. Top with nuts or coconut.
6. Keep refrigerated.

Susan Toups Clement

SPICED FIG CAKE WITH CREOLE CREAM CHEESE BUTTERCREAM

Serves: 8 to 10

ICING

8 ounces heavy cream

2 (8 ounce) packages cream cheese

4 ounces sour cream

4 ounces butter

1 tablespoon vanilla extract

4 cups powdered sugar

pecans or walnuts, toasted (optional)

CAKE

1 cup sugar

½ cup butter, softened to
   room temperature

2 eggs

½ cup buttermilk

1 teaspoon baking soda (dissolved in
   the buttermilk)

1 (8 ounce) jar of your favorite fig preserves

2 cups all-purpose flour

¼ teaspoon cloves

1 teaspoon allspice

1 teaspoon cinnamon

½ teaspoon ground ginger

Chef Brandon Naquin

1. To make icing, whip heavy cream to stiff peak and reserve.

2. Cream together cream cheese, sour cream and butter, scraping the bowl.

3. Add vanilla extract, and slowly add the powdered sugar to form the icing.

4. Fold in the whipped heavy cream to lighten the icing.

5. Refrigerate for 30 minutes.

6. Preheat oven to 350 degrees.

7. Cream together sugar and butter.

8. Add eggs, buttermilk with soda and fig preserves.

9. In a separate bowl, mix flour, cloves, allspice, cinnamon and ginger and slowly stir into the wet ingredients, mix well.

10. Pour into 2 greased and flour dusted 8 inch round or square cake pans.

11. Bake for 30 to 35 minutes until brown, then remove from oven.

12. Once cakes are completely cooled remove from cake pans.

13. Place 1 cake on desired serving platter.

14. Apply a generous layer of icing, taking care to spread the icing evenly to the edge of the cake.

15. Invert the remaining cake so that the "bottom" of the cake is now the top.

16. Gently press the cake onto the icing of the bottom layer of cake, centering the layers.

17. Top with icing and smooth the top and sides with remaining icing.

18. If desired, crust the outside of the cake with toasted nuts, pecans or walnuts.

OUTDOOR BARBECUE

GRILLED SQUASH SALAD

Serves: 6 to 8

Refreshingly light. Great summer side.

2 zucchini, sliced lengthwise

2 yellow squash, sliced lengthwise

salt and pepper, to taste

olive oil

1 cup mayonnaise

1 boiled egg, finely chopped

1 teaspoon Dijon mustard

juice and zest of 1 lemon

1 stalk celery, peeled and thinly diced

½ sweet onion, thinly diced

½ bunch green onions, finely chopped

1 tablespoon parsley, chopped

salt and pepper, to taste

Tabasco sauce, to taste

1. Season zucchini and squash with salt and pepper and lightly toss in oil.
2. Grill or roast at high temperature in oven until nicely colored and juicy.
3. Cut into chunks.
4. Mix mayonnaise, egg, mustard, lemon juice and zest, celery, onions and parsley for dressing.
5. Toss zucchini and squash with enough dressing to coat.
6. Add salt, pepper and Tabasco to taste.
7. Can be served warm or cold.

Scott Harang

CLASSIC BBQ SAUCE

Serves: 3 cups

1 cup ketchup

¼ cup plus 2 tablespoons water

¼ cup plus 1 tablespoon cider vinegar

¼ cup plus 1 tablespoon white vinegar

¼ tablespoon plus 1 ½ teaspoons brown sugar

2 tablespoons plus 1 ½ teaspoons Worcestershire sauce

1 tablespoon chili powder

1 tablespoon ground cumin

1 ½ teaspoons kosher salt

1 ½ teaspoons coarse black pepper

1. Combine all ingredients in a pot.

2. Warm gently over medium heat, without bringing to a boil, stirring occasionally, for approximately 5 minutes.

3. Brush over chicken or your favorite grilled protein.

Susan Stagni

CAM'S BARBECUE CRABS

Serves: 24 crabs

2 dozen live crabs

2 sticks butter, melted

juice of 1 lemon

½ cup Italian dressing

1 tablespoon Worcestershire sauce

1 teaspoon garlic powder

1 teaspoon paprika

¼ teaspoon cayenne pepper

1 tablespoon BBQ sauce

1. To prepare the crabs, place live crabs in ice water to stun.

2. Once stunned, remove the top shell of the crab by inserting a knife into the abdomen and prying open.

3. Remove and discard the gills and organs.

4. Leave the legs, claws, crab cavity and crabmeat.

5. To make sauce, combine melted butter, lemon juice, Italian dressing, Worcestershire sauce, garlic powder, paprika, cayenne pepper and BBQ sauce.

6. Preheat grill to medium high heat and place crabs with cavity facing upwards.

7. Baste crabs generously with sauce.

8. Total cooking time depends on size of the crabs and the heat of the grill, but takes approximately 10 to 20 minutes.

9. Continue basting.

10. Crabs are done when sauce bubbles in the shell, sauce is caramelized and the bottom of the crab shell is lightly charred.

Camile Chiasson

CAM'S BARBECUE RIBS

Serves: 4 to 6

1 **package bone in pork loin back ribs, washed and patted dry**

2 **tablespoons Tony Chachere's seasoning**

1 **tablespoon garlic salt**

1 **tablespoon Worcestershire sauce**

2 **tablespoons olive oil**

1 **cup Sweet Baby Ray's barbeque sauce**

1. The night before barbecuing, cut each rib into 3 equal sections so the ribs are easier to handle on the grill.

2. Season ribs generously with Tony Chachere's seasoning, garlic salt, Worcestershire sauce and olive oil and marinate in refrigerator over night.

3. Remove from refrigerator an hour or so before grilling, allowing to reach room temperature.

4. Preheat oven to 300 degrees and pit to 450 degrees.

5. Sear ribs on pit on both sides.

6. Remove from pit and bake in oven for 1 ½ hours.

7. Remove from oven and discard pan drippings.

8. Put ribs back on pit over low fire or indirect heat (approximately 200 to 250 degrees) for another hour.

9. When meat starts to fall off the bone, baste with barbecue sauce on both sides.

10. Cook for additional 10 minutes or until sauce caramelizes on the ribs.

Camile Chiasson

DRUNKEN CHICKEN

Serves: 2 to 4

1 whole frying chicken

1 tablespoon sesame oil

Louisiana Hot Sauce

salt and pepper, to taste

season-all, to taste

1 (12 ounce) can beer

1 tablespoon Worcestershire sauce

1 tablespoon Tiger Sauce

1 tablespoon teriyaki sauce

1 tablespoon honey

salt and pepper, to taste

season-all, to taste

Greek seasoning, to taste

1. Preheat grill to 425 degrees.

2. Rub down chicken with sesame oil and Louisiana Hot Sauce and then sprinkle with salt, pepper and season-all.

3. Next, open beer can, pour out half and add Worcestershire sauce, Tiger Sauce, teriyaki sauce, honey, salt, pepper, season-all and Greek seasoning (to fill up appoximately ¾ of the can).

4. Set the chicken on top of the beer can and make sure it is stable.

5. Place the chicken on the grill with direct heat at approximately 425 to 450 degrees.

6. Turn every 5 to 10 minutes to make sure it is evenly cooking.

7. After 30 minutes turn off 1 of the burners, move the chicken to that side of grill and cook for approximately 90 to 120 additional minutes.

8. Carefully remove chicken from grill and top with sauce from beer can.

Patrick Ellender and David Elias

POOLSIDE PARTY

Your guests will love this classic poolside spread.
This menu is simple, easy to prepare and a crowd
pleaser for kids and adults.

— MENU —

SUMMER MEAT AND CHEESE TRAY

FRESH SQUEEZED LEMONADE AND THE FESTIVAL

BOURGEOIS BEST BIG BURGERS, ASIAN COLESLAW,
ALUMNI GRILL PEPPER JAC MAC

LEMON ALMOND TART WITH SUMMER BERRIES

SUMMER MEAT AND CHEESE TRAY

Serves: 8

Estimate 1 to 2 ounces of cheese and meat per person. Use 5 different cheeses and approximately 1 meat to every 2 cheeses. Cheese platter can be prepared several hours ahead of time and stored in the refrigerator.

1 cup walnuts, chopped

2 tablespoons honey

6 ounces blackberries

¼ cup water

¼ cup sugar

sprig of rosemary

8 ounces Brie cheese

8 ounces manchego cheese, cut into cubes

8 ounces Gorgonzola cheese

8 ounces Gouda cheese

8 ounces drunken goat cheese

5 ounces dry coppa (pork shoulder)

5 ounces calabrese salame

honey

kiwi

grapes

strawberries

blueberries

pistachios

olives or cornichons

2 kinds of crackers

1. To make honey walnuts, combine chopped walnuts and 2 tablespoons honey in mixing bowl and stir until evenly coated.

2. To make blackberry sauce, place blackberries, water, sugar and rosemary in a pot and bring to a boil.

3. Simmer on low heat for 20 to 25 minutes.

4. Let cool to room temperature.

5. On a large serving platter, place cheeses first and then build around them.

6. Next arrange the meats by folding/rolling them to create texture.

7. Fill a small bowl with honey and another small bowl with blackberry sauce and place them on the platter.

8. Last, position the fruit, nuts and olives or cornichons to fill in any open space on the platter.

9. Serve with crackers on a separate plate, so that cheese plate can be refrigerated until ready to serve.

Julie Bernard Robichaux

FRESH SQUEEZED LEMONADE

Serves: 10 to 12

1 ¾ cups sugar

8 cups water

1 ½ cups fresh lemon juice
(approximately 16 to 20 lemons)

1. Boil the sugar and 1 cup of water, then cool to room temperature.
2. Cover and chill.
3. Stir together chilled syrup, lemon juice and 7 cups of water.
4. Serve over ice.

Renee B Biondo

THE FESTIVAL

Serves: 1 drink

1 to 2 fresh Louisiana strawberries

¼ ounce simple syrup

1 to 2 fresh mint leaves

2 ounces vodka

3 ounces fresh squeezed lemonade

strawberry, to garnish

mint, to garnish

1. Muddle strawberries at the bottom of a shaker with simple syrup.
2. Add mint leaves on top and fill with ice.
3. Pour in vodka and lemonade and shake well.
4. Strain into glass with crushed ice and garnish with strawberry and/or mint.

Donner-Peltier Distillers

BOURGEOIS
MEAT MARKET

BOURGEOIS BEST BIG BURGERS

Serves: 8

Bourgeois Meat Market, established in 1891, is a local favorite, known world-wide, for its beef jerky. These burgers are made with Bourgeois ground meat and sausage only. The ground meat and sausage combination is so delicious and perfectly seasoned that no additional seasoning is necessary.

2 pounds Bourgeois fresh sausage (recommend jalapeno)

2 pounds Bourgeois ground meat

1 pound pepper jack cheese

8 large hamburger buns (recommend sesame seed)

onions, grilled (optional)

bacon, cooked (optional)

lettuce, shredded (optional)

tomatoes, sliced (optional)

1. Preheat grill to medium high heat.
2. Remove fresh sausage from the casing and mix with ground meat by hand.
3. Make 8 half pound burgers by patting the meat back and forth in your hands until the desired thickness is attained (thinner and wider is better).
4. Add the burgers to a hot charcoal grill and cook thoroughly.
5. Add cheese to the burgers right before they are done cooking to melt.
6. Serve hamburgers on sesame seed buns and top with onions, bacon, lettuce and/or tomatoes, if desired.

Bourgeois Meat Market

ASIAN COLESLAW

Serves: 6 to 8

To make ahead, prepare salad mix, almond/noodle mixture and dressing. Combine right before serving.

COLESLAW

1 pack Ramen noodles (any flavor)

1 cup almonds, slivered

2 bags coleslaw, shredded

3 to 4 stalks green onions, chopped

DRESSING

½ cup red wine vinegar

½ cup olive oil

½ cup sugar

1 pack Ramen noodle seasoning packet

1. Preheat oven to 350 degrees.

2. While oven is preheating, crush Ramen noodles into small pieces (can put in a zip lock bag and hit with the end of a spoon to crush).

3. Set Ramen seasoning packet to the side.

4. After Ramen noodles are crushed, spread Ramen noodles and slivered almonds on cookie sheet.

5. Toast in oven for approximately 5 to 7 minutes checking to make sure they are not burning.

6. Pour coleslaw into a large bowl and place green onions on top.

7. After Ramen noodles and almonds are done baking, let cool and then pour on top of coleslaw and green onions.

8. To make dressing, in large mason jar or shaker, combine red wine vinegar, olive oil, sugar and Ramen noodle seasoning packet.

9. Pour dressing on top of coleslaw mixture before serving.

Katie L Bilello

CHEF MINH LE

HOMETOWN:

Houma, Louisiana

EDUCATION AND EXPERIENCE:

Chef Minh Le earned a Bachelor of Science Degree in Culinary Arts from Nicholls State University. He has over 25 years of food service experience in hotels and local restaurants. Chef Minh Le is now the owner and Executive Chef of Alumni Grill in Thibodaux.

"My favorite things about Thibodaux are the wonderful and friendly people of the community that I have gotten to know, the many events that take place each year that brings the community together and great fishing in the surrounding area."

ALUMNI GRILL PEPPER JACK MAC

Serves: 4 to 6

1 pound elbow macaroni

1 ounce butter

1 ounce flour

½ teaspoon garlic powder

½ teaspoon onion powder

½ teaspoon crushed red pepper

1 teaspoon salt

3 cups milk

1 cup heavy cream

1 egg yolk

12 ounces Cheddar cheese, grated and divided

20 ounces pepper jack cheese, grated and divided

1. Preheat oven to 350 degrees.
2. Cook pasta according to directions on box and set aside.
3. In a pot over medium heat, melt butter and add flour to make a white roux.
4. Whisk in garlic powder, onion powder, crushed red pepper and salt. Then, add milk, heavy cream and egg yolk.
5. Whisk and cook sauce until it thickens to heavy cream consistency.
6. Add 4 ounces Cheddar cheese and 12 ounces pepper jack cheese, stir until melted.
7. Remove from heat and pour over cooked pasta.
8. Top with remaining Cheddar and pepper jack cheese and bake for 10 minutes or until cheese is melted.

Chef Minh Le

LEMON ALMOND TART WITH SUMMER BERRIES

Serves: 6

Delicious recipe for a special occasion. Almond paste can be found in the specialty baking section of your local supermarket.

LEMON CURD (MICROWAVE)

1 tablespoon zest and juice of 3 lemons

¼ cup unsalted butter, softened

1 cup sugar

2 eggs

ALMOND TART CRUST

75 vanilla wafers (recommend Jack's), finely crushed

2 ounces almonds, slivered

¼ cup powdered sugar

½ cup butter, melted

FILLING

1 (7 ounce) pack almond paste

2 eggs

¼ cup sugar

2 tablespoons butter, melted

2/3 cup lemon curd

summer berries (blueberries, raspberries, blackberries), to garnish

créme fraiche, to garnish

1. To make lemon curd, zest lemons to make 1 tablespoon of zest.
2. Cut lemons and squeeze juice into measuring cup to equal ½ cup.
3. Using 3 quart glass/microwave safe bowl, beat together butter and sugar with electric mixer until blended.
4. Add eggs 1 at a time, beating until just blended.
5. Gradually add lemon juice to butter mixture, beating at low speed after each addition.
6. Stir in lemon zest.
7. Microwave on high for 5 minutes, stirring at 1 minute intervals.
8. Continue to microwave, stirring at 30 second intervals, until mixture thickens and coats back of spoon.
9. Place heavy duty plastic wrap directly on top of warm curd.
10. Chill for a minimum of 4 hours until firm.
11. Can store in airtight container for up to 2 weeks in refrigerator.
12. To make the crust, preheat oven to 350 degrees.
13. Pulse wafers in food processor.
14. Add almonds and pulse several times until coarsely chopped when mixed with wafer crumbs.
15. Add powdered sugar and pulse to mix.
16. Slowly add melted butter to processor bowl.

Jean B Ayo

17. Press crumb mixture on bottom and sides of 6 greased 4 inch tart pans with removable bottoms.

18. Place on baking sheet.

19. Bake 10 to 12 minutes until lightly browned.

20. To make the filling, decrease oven temperature to 325 degrees.

21. Beat almond paste, eggs, sugar, butter and lemon curd until well blended.

22. Pour mixture into crusts, bake for 15 to 20 minutes until set and brown around the edges.

23. Cool 30 minutes.

24. Cover and chill 1 to 24 hours.

25. Remove tarts from pans, top with fresh berries and créme fraiche.

FALL

The fall season means back to "the grind"— kids are in school,
weeknights are busy, weekends are filled with sports and tailgating,
local sugarcane is being harvested and oysters are in season.

── IN SEASON ──

ACORN SQUASH	CAULIFLOWER	PECANS
ARUGULA	CRANBERRIES	PUMPKINS
BROCCOLI	GRAPES	SPINACH
BRUSSELS SPROUTS	MIRLITON	SWEET POTATOES
BUTTERNUT SQUASH	MUSHROOMS	TURNIPS
	PEARS	

BREAKFAST DISHES

Start the morning off right with these hearty dishes.

COLD COFFEE PUNCH

Serves:
approximately 15

Would be a great addition to any brunch—takes cold brew coffee to another level.

½ gallon of vanilla ice cream

1 (12 ounce) original cool brew
   coffee concentrate

1 (12 ounce) vanilla cool brew
   coffee concentrate

1 quart half and half

sugar, to taste

1. Melt ice cream.
2. Pour coffee and half and half over the ice cream.
3. Whisk ingredients together.
4. Keep cold.
5. Add sugar if needed.

Sunday Gilly

ALMOND BISCOTTI

Serves:
approximately 40 pieces

Great to dip in coffee, especially the cold coffee punch.

1 cup almonds, sliced

1 cup almonds, slivered

4 to 4 ½ cups flour

1 tablespoon baking powder

½ teaspoon salt

1 cup butter

2 cups sugar

4 eggs

1 tablespoon vanilla extract

zest from 1 lemon

Brigid Grace Himel

1. Preheat oven to 275 degrees.

2. Toast all almonds for 5 to 7 minutes. Remove to cool.

3. Increase heat to 325 degrees and grease 2 large sheet pans.

4. Combine 4 cups of flour, baking powder and salt; set aside.

5. In a stand mixer, using the flat paddle attachment, beat butter and sugar until fluffy.

6. Add 3 eggs, 1 at a time.

7. Separate fourth egg, add just the yolk and vanilla extract to butter mix and beat. With the mixer on low, add dry ingredients.

8. Stir in lemon zest and toasted nuts with a spoon.

9. If dough won't shape, add more flour.

10. To prevent stickiness, use wet or greased hands. Divide into 4 pieces. Roll each into 14 inch by 2 ½ inch logs, placing 2 logs on each cookie sheet.

11. Cook 25 to 30 minutes until firm and golden, switching racks halfway through.

12. Remove from oven and let cool for 10 minutes.

13. Decrease temperature to 250 degrees.

14. Spritz logs with lukewarm water and cut with serrated knife on the diagonal in ½ inch slices.

15. Place sliced biscotti flat on baking sheet and bake until dry and toasted, approximately 15 to 20 minutes.

16. Cool individually on wire racks.

BANANA NUT BREAD

Serves: 6 to 8

BREAD

3 cups Pioneer Biscuit Mix

1 cup brown sugar

1 cup milk

¼ cup butter

2 eggs

3 bananas, mashed

1 cup pecans, chopped

GLAZE (OPTIONAL)

¼ cup butter

¼ cup milk

1 teaspoon vanilla extract

2 cups powdered sugar

1. Preheat oven to 350 degrees.

2. Combine biscuit mix, brown sugar, milk, butter and eggs and mix well.

3. Add bananas and pecans and mix until well blended.

4. Pour into a well-greased and floured Bundt pan (or 3 small loaf pans).

5. Bake for 40 to 45 minutes.

6. To make glaze, in small saucepan, melt butter with milk and vanilla extract.

7. Remove from stove and add powdered sugar.

8. Beat well and pour over cake while still warm or simply top with powdered sugar.

Terri Robertson

BEIGNETS

Serves: 16 to 20

Remember to make the dough the night before! Check out the Cajun Ninja's YouTube Channel for step-by-step instructions on how to make these beignets.

1 (0.25 ounce) packet active dry yeast

½ cup lukewarm water

½ cup sugar

6 cups all-purpose flour

1 teaspoon salt

8 ounces cream cheese, softened

½ cup salted butter, softened

3 eggs

1 cup whole milk

vegetable oil

powdered sugar, to garnish

Jason Derouen, The Cajun Ninja

1. Activate dry yeast by adding packet to lukewarm water and dissolve for 10 minutes.

2. In a large bowl, combine sugar, flour and salt; mix well with a fork.

3. Add cream cheese, butter, eggs, milk and yeast and water mixture to the dry ingredients. Combine using hands until all ingredients have been blended well.

4. Place dough on a pan, cover with saran wrap and leave in refrigerator overnight to rise.

5. In the morning, heat 1 ½ inches of vegetable oil in a frying pan on high.

6. Pound and roll out dough on a lightly floured surface. Roll dough to ¼ inch thickness, trim edges and cut into squares.

7. Fry dough squares in heated oil, turning beignets when dough browns and puffs up.

8. Remove from oil, place on paper towel to remove excess oil and sprinkle with powdered sugar.

BREAKFAST CASSEROLE

Serves: 12

May be made ahead and refrigerated overnight for a holiday or weekend morning.

1 pound maple breakfast sausage

1 (30 ounce) package frozen cubed hash browns with onions and peppers

12 large eggs

1 tablespoon milk

2 cups Cheddar cheese, shredded

¼ bunch of green onions, finely chopped

1. Preheat oven to 350 degrees.

2. In a large skillet, cook sausage over medium heat, stirring until sausage crumbles and is no longer pink. Drain well.

3. Grease a 9 x 13 inch casserole dish and add hash browns and sausage.

4. In a bowl, whisk together eggs and milk. Pour evenly over potato mixture.

5. Add cheese to the top. Sprinkle with green onions.

6. Bake for 35 to 40 minutes. If refrigerated, bake for an hour.

Casey Guidry

WEEKNIGHT MEALS

Try these quick and easy kid-friendly meals on
those busy weeknights.

TACO SOUP

Serves: 6 to 8

Can add extra ground meat for a heartier meal.

1 pound lean ground meat

1 onion, chopped

1 (0.4 ounce) package ranch salad dressing
and seasoning mix

1 (1 ounce) package taco seasoning mix

1 (11 ounce) can Mexican corn

1 (15 ounce) can ranch style chili beans

1 (15 ounce) can pinto beans

1 (15 ounce) can black beans

2 (4.5 ounce) cans green chiles, chopped

2 (10 ounce) cans mild Rotel

1 (8 ounce) can tomato sauce

taco chips (optional)

sour cream (optional)

black olives (optional)

lettuce (optional)

shredded cheese (optional)

1. In a skillet, brown ground meat with onion. Drain excess grease.

2. Pour all other ingredients into a soup pot and add cooked ground meat.

3. Cook 1 to 2 hours on low, stirring frequently. This recipe can also be done in the crockpot.

4. Serve with taco chips, sour cream, black olives, lettuce and shredded cheese, as desired.

Debbie Frey

WHITE CHICKEN CHILI

Serves: 4

For a healthier version, substitute Greek yogurt for sour cream.

1 onion, diced

2 cloves garlic, minced

1 tablespoon olive oil

1 jalapeno, seeded and chopped

1 (15 ounce) can Great Northern beans, drained

1 (4 ounce) can green chiles, chopped

3 green onions, chopped

1 ½ teaspoons cumin

½ teaspoon dried oregano

1 teaspoon salt

¼ teaspoon pepper

2 cups chicken broth

1 tablespoon lime juice

1 cup water

¼ cup milk

1 tablespoon flour

1 pound chicken, cooked and cubed (can also use a rotisserie chicken)

¼ cup sour cream

shredded cheese

1. Sauté onion and garlic in olive oil until browned.

2. Add jalapeno, beans, chiles, green onions, cumin, oregano, salt, pepper, broth, lime juice and water; bring to a boil.

3. Reduce heat to medium and simmer for approximately 20 minutes.

4. In a bowl, whisk milk and flour and then add to the chili.

5. Add chicken and sour cream and simmer for 5 to 10 minutes.

6. Top with shredded cheese and serve hot.

Katherine Toups Elias

CHILI

Serves: 6 to 8

You can use any kind of ground meat in your freezer for this one.

2 pounds ground beef

6 tablespoons olive oil, divided

½ large onion, chopped

½ bell pepper, diced

½ jalapeno pepper, chopped

3 cloves garlic, minced

1 tomato, diced

2 teaspoons salt

¼ teaspoon cayenne pepper

¼ teaspoon coarse black pepper

1 tablespoon Louisiana Hot Sauce

3 ounces tomato paste

1 (15 ounce) can tomato sauce

3 tablespoons chili powder

¼ teaspoon cumin

1 tablespoon cornstarch

¼ cup water

1. Brown beef in 3 tablespoons olive oil. Drain off excess oil.

2. In a separate pot, brown onion, bell pepper, jalapeno pepper and garlic in remaining 3 tablespoons olive oil.

3. To the vegetables, add tomato, salt, cayenne pepper, black pepper, Louisiana Hot Sauce, tomato paste and tomato sauce.

4. Cook for 45 minutes on low, stirring occasionally, then combine with ground meat.

5. Add chili powder and cumin.

6. Dissolve corn starch with ¼ cup water and add to the other ingredients.

7. Cook all together for 30 minutes. Add additional water if desired.

Melanie Delaune and Melissa Clement,
in memory of Eldon "Plucker" Clement

CROCKPOT BARBECUED BEEF

Serves: 6 to 8

1 (4 pound) boneless pot roast, lean chuck, rump roast or top round

½ cup of water

1 ½ cups ketchup

1 ¼ cups of Dr. Pepper or Coke

2 tablespoons mustard

3 tablespoons Worcestershire sauce

¼ teaspoon Tabasco sauce

1. Put roast in slow cooker with water.
2. Cover and cook on low for 10 to 12 hours or high for 6 hours.
3. Once cooked, remove roast and shred with fork. Discard fat. If desired, drain juices.
4. Return to crockpot and stir in ketchup, cola, mustard, Worcestershire and Tabasco sauce.
5. Cover and cook on high for 1 hour.
6. Serve alone or on buns.

Neely Newchurch

HEALTHY CABBAGE SALAD

Serves: 12

1 medium head of cabbage

2 medium cloves of garlic, mashed

1 teaspoon salt

pinch of dry mint

dash of pepper

1 tablespoon Greek seasoning

½ cup lemon juice

1 ½ tablespoons balsamic vinegar

1 ½ tablespoons olive oil

1. Wash and drain cabbage, then shred.
2. In a mason jar, mix garlic with salt and mint and add pepper and Greek seasoning.
3. Add lemon juice, vinegar and olive oil and mix well.
4. Pour over cabbage and toss to combine.

Marcie Elias

LOUISIANA RED BEANS

Serves: 6 to 8

The oil in this recipe adds depth and makes this dish special.

1 pound red beans, washed, drained,
   soaked in water overnight and drained

3 cups cold water

2 cloves garlic, chopped

½ cup celery, chopped

1 large bay leaf, crushed

1 medium onion, chopped

½ cup cooking oil

salt and pepper, to taste

1 pound smoked sausage, sliced

2 tablespoons parsley, chopped

cooked rice

1. Place beans in cold water in a 4 quart pot.
2. Add garlic, celery, bay leaf, onion and oil and bring to a boil.
3. Reduce heat and simmer for approximately 2 hours. Add water as needed, stirring occasionally.
4. Add salt, pepper, sausage and parsley and continue cooking over low heat for approximately 1 hour.
5. Serve over hot rice.

1982 Louisiana Legacy Cookbook

RICE COOKER JAMBALAYA

Serves: 12 to 15

3 cups white or brown rice

½ cup butter

1 pound smoked sausage, chopped

1 cooked chicken, deboned

1 (10 ounce) can mild or original Rotel

1 (14.5 ounce) can chicken or beef broth

1 (10.5 ounce) can French onion soup

1 cup water

1 teaspoon Kitchen Bouquet

1 teaspoon Cajun seasoning

1 teaspoon garlic powder

1 teaspoon onion powder

1. Combine all ingredients in a large rice cooker and stir.
2. Cook on correct setting for type of rice used.
3. Note: Ensure your rice cooker can hold 20 cups of cooked rice.
4. Serve hot.

Kristi B Gravois

SET AND FORGET CHICKEN STEW

Serves: 6 to 8

3 pounds chicken (recommend boneless chicken thighs)

Tony Chachere's seasoning, to taste

1 small onion, chopped

1 small bell pepper, chopped

1 (10.5 ounce) can cream of celery soup

1 (10.5 ounce) can golden mushroom soup

1 (6 ounce) can mushroom steak sauce

2 (1 ounce) packets brown gravy mix

cooked rice

1. Clean chicken and season with Tony Chachere's.
2. Place all ingredients except rice in a slow cooker and cook on low for 4 to 6 hours.
3. Serve over hot rice.

Renee B Biondo

POTATO AND SMOKED
SAUSAGE STEW

Serves: 8 to 10

This is an easy one pot comfort meal.

1 cup canola oil

1 cup all-purpose flour

1 onion, diced

1 bunch green onions, sliced

1 bunch Italian parsley, chopped

3 cloves garlic, chopped

1 pound smoked sausage, sliced

1 pound red potatoes, diced

salt and pepper, to taste

1 to 2 quart(s) chicken broth or water

cooked rice (optional)

1. In a large Dutch oven, heat canola oil on medium heat and add flour to make a roux.

2. Stir constantly until the roux is medium brown.

3. Add onion, green onions, parsley, garlic and sausage.

4. Sauté in roux until onions are translucent and sausage starts to render, approximately 8 to 10 minutes.

5. Add potatoes, salt, pepper and just enough chicken broth or water to cover the ingredients.

6. Cover pot and cook on low until potatoes are tender, 30 to 40 minutes, stirring often.

7. Can serve over hot rice.

Chef Jarred Zeringue

CHEF JARRED ZERINGUE

HOMETOWN:

Vacherie, Louisiana

EDUCATION AND EXPERIENCE:

Chef Jarred learned what he knows about cooking in the kitchens of his mother and grandmothers. Chef Jarred founded Eat New Orleans, Vacherie and Café Conti and now owns Wayne Jacob's Smokehouse and Restaurant located in LaPlace, Louisiana.

"I love all of the local and authentic Cajun places to eat in Thibodaux that I remember from my childhood. I love that the local culture celebrates around food and cooking."

OYSTER SPAGHETTI

Serves: 6

6 tablespoons extra virgin olive oil

6 tablespoons butter

3 tablespoons garlic, minced

1 teaspoon crushed red pepper flakes

4 dozen large oysters, drained but not rinsed

½ cup dry white wine

1 pound spaghetti

3 tablespoons flat leaf parsley, chopped

Parmesan cheese, grated

1. In a Dutch oven, heat oil and butter over medium low heat until melted.
2. Add garlic and cook until golden, being careful not to burn.
3. Add crushed red pepper flakes and cook for 1 minute.
4. Add oysters and wine and cook for 5 to 10 minutes.
5. While this is cooking, cook spaghetti according to package directions.
6. Add the parsley to oysters and stir.
7. Combine cooked spaghetti with oysters and sauce.
8. Divide into 6 pasta plates or shallow bowls and sprinkle with Parmesan cheese. Serve immediately.

Casey Guidry

JALAPENO CHICKEN

Serves: 10 to 12

4 tablespoons butter or margarine

1 cup onions, chopped

2 green jalapeno peppers, chopped

1 pint sour cream

2 (10.5 ounce) cans cream of chicken soup

4 green onions, chopped

1 (10 ounce) box frozen chopped spinach, cooked and drained

2 teaspoons salt

4 ounces tortilla chips

6 cups cooked chicken, chopped (approximately 2 rotisserie chickens)

8 ounces Monterey Jack cheese, grated

1. Preheat oven to 350 degrees.

2. In a 3 quart saucepan, melt butter and sauté onions until wilted, but not brown.

3. Add jalapenos, sour cream, chicken soup, green onions, spinach and salt. Mix well.

4. Layer unbroken tortilla chips in the bottom of a greased 9 x 13 x 2 inch dish.

5. Add the chopped chicken.

6. Cover well with sauce and top with grated cheese.

7. Bake for 1 hour.

1982 Louisiana Legacy Cookbook

JOHNNY JAMBALAYA'S BAYOU CHICKEN

Serves: 4

This dish was one of the most popular dishes at the Country Club's Johnny Jambalaya's Bayou Bistro.

4 thin-cut chicken breasts

½ to ¾ cup Johnny Jambalaya's Herb Dressing and Marinade

4 tablespoons olive oil, divided

1 onion, sliced

1 bell pepper, sliced

4 slices bacon, halved

4 slices pepper jack cheese

1. Marinate chicken breasts overnight in enough herb dressing to evenly coat the chicken breasts. Take the chicken out of the refrigerator approximately 1 hour prior to cooking.

2. Preheat oven to 375 degrees.

3. In a skillet, heat 2 tablespoons olive oil over medium high heat.

4. Once hot, sauté onion and bell pepper in the oil until soft and slightly caramelized. Set aside.

5. In a cast iron skillet, heat remaining 2 tablespoons olive oil on high heat.

6. Once hot, add chicken breasts and sear, approximately 2 minutes on each side.

7. Once chicken breasts are seared, turn off heat, add 2 halves of bacon to the top of each chicken breast and put in oven for 15 to 20 minutes.

8. Take the chicken out, top with onion and bell pepper mixture and pepper jack cheese.

9. Return to oven and allow the cheese to melt.

10. Once cheese is melted, remove from oven and serve with garlic green beans.

Mandy Percle Broussard

JOHNNY JAMBALAYA'S GARLIC GREEN BEANS

Serves: 4

1 tablespoon olive oil

3 to 4 handfuls fresh green beans,
  rinsed and ends snapped

salt and pepper, to taste

6 cloves garlic, minced

2 tablespoons soy sauce

1. Heat olive oil in a skillet over medium heat.

2. Once hot, add green beans and sauté in the pan.

3. Season with salt and pepper.

4. Once green beans are softened, add minced
    garlic, allowing garlic to become aromatic.

5. Once green beans are to desired softness, add
    soy sauce and stir to combine.

Mandy Percle Broussard

CROCKPOT POT PIE

Serves: 8

1 ½ pounds boneless, skinless chicken breasts, cut into 1 inch pieces

2 cups carrots, chopped

1 medium onion, diced

2 stalks celery, chopped

1 (8 ounce) can water chestnuts, drained

1 to 2 cup(s) frozen peas

1 (10.75 ounce) can condensed cream of chicken soup

1 (10.75 ounce) can condensed cream of celery soup

1 ½ cups chicken broth

1 teaspoon thyme

¼ teaspoon pepper

1 (6 ounce) can biscuits, cut into bite-sized pieces

1. Place chicken, carrots, onion, celery, water chestnuts and peas in crockpot.

2. In a separate bowl, combine chicken soup, celery soup, chicken broth, thyme and pepper and mix well.

3. Pour into crockpot and mix.

4. Cook on low heat for 7 to 8 hours.

5. At the end of cooking, raise heat to high, add biscuit pieces and cook for approximately 30 minutes or until dough is cooked through.

Jamie Mutter

CAJUN STYLE MEATLOAF

Serves: 12 to 15

This is an interesting twist on traditional meatloaf for egg lovers.
Hearty meal that can be eaten all week.

MEATLOAF

6 eggs

3 pounds ground beef or sirloin

1 pound ground pork

¼ cup water

1 ½ cups Italian style breadcrumbs

1 teaspoon all-purpose seasoned salt

1 tablespoon Worcestershire sauce

1 tablespoon garlic powder

1 tablespoon onion powder

1 teaspoon salt

1 teaspoon pepper

1 tablespoon ketchup

2 tablespoons mayonnaise

GRAVY

2 (1 ounce) packages dry brown gravy mix,
   prepare according to package

1 (1 ounce) package Au Jus dry gravy mix,
   prepare according to package

1 (12 ounce) can or jar beef gravy

1 (8 ounce) can tomato sauce

1 (10.5 ounce) can French onion soup

8 ounces mushrooms, fresh or canned,
   sliced and drained

1. Preheat oven to 350 degrees.

2. Boil and peel 2 eggs.

3. Spray an 11 x 14 inch pan with non-stick spray. Combine ground beef and pork with fork.

4. Add remaining ingredients except the boiled eggs and mix by hand.

5. Pat meat mixture into pan and shape for baking.

6. Using your hands, make 2 small indentions on top of meatloaf about 3 inches apart to place the boiled eggs. Make sure to cover the eggs with the meat.

7. Cover meatloaf with aluminum foil and bake for 45 minutes to 1 hour.

8. Remove from oven and drain grease.

9. While meatloaf is baking, mix all gravy ingredients together on stove for approximately 5 minutes. Pour gravy mixture on top of meatloaf while baking. There will be leftover gravy at this point. Re-cover and continue to bake for another hour.

10. Remove foil and baste meatloaf with gravy.

11. Bake uncovered for 20 to 30 minutes until brown.

12. Serve over mashed potatoes or spaghetti with additional gravy. Leftover gravy freezes well.

Sue C Blakeman

MEATBALLS IN BROWN GRAVY

Serves: 14 to 16

Meatballs and gravy may be served over steaming rice, but it is best over spaghetti, topped with Parmesan cheese. Petit pois add a nice finishing touch as a side dish. This freezes well and leftovers make delicious po-boys!

MEATBALLS

2 ½ to 3 pounds ground beef

1 pound lean ground pork

3 teaspoons salt

½ teaspoon red pepper

½ teaspoon black pepper

1 tablespoon ketchup

1/3 cup onion, finely chopped

2 slices broken white bread, soaked in 2/3 cup milk

1/3 cup oatmeal

½ cup flour

½ cup vegetable oil

BROWN GRAVY

½ cup oil

¾ cup flour

1 large onion, finely chopped

½ green pepper, finely chopped

2 cloves garlic, finely chopped

5 to 6 cups hot water

1 (14.5 ounce) can beef broth (optional)

1. To make meatballs, place all ingredients, except flour and vegetable oil, in a large bowl and mix together well.

2. Form balls of desired size, approximately 3 dozen.

3. Roll lightly in flour.

4. Cover bottom of large skillet with vegetable oil, heat to medium and brown meatballs on all sides.

5. Remove from skillet and drain on paper towels.

6. To prepare gravy, make a roux with oil and flour.

7. When roux becomes a dark brown color, add onion, pepper and garlic.

8. Sauté until tender, then add hot water and beef broth.

9. Allow this mixture to boil for 15 to 20 minutes, stirring occasionally.

10. Add meatballs and reduce heat to medium.

11. Cover and cook for 1 hour. Add water if needed to thin gravy to desired consistency, stirring occasionally.

Tateen Ory
1982 Louisiana Legacy Cookbook

DEANNA AND CARROLL'S PEPPERONI LASAGNA

Serves: 10 to 12

1 pound mild or hot breakfast sausage

6 ounces pepperoni, finely ground

1 clove garlic, minced

1 tablespoon dry basil

1 ½ teaspoons salt

1 (16 ounce) can petite diced tomatoes

2 (6 ounce) cans tomato paste

10 ounces lasagna noodles

3 cups fresh ricotta or creamy cottage cheese

½ cup Romano cheese, grated

2 tablespoons parsley flakes

2 eggs, beaten

1 teaspoon salt

½ teaspoon black pepper

1 pound mozzarella cheese, shredded

1. Preheat oven to 375 degrees.
2. Brown sausage and drain excess fat.
3. Add pepperoni, garlic, basil, salt, diced tomatoes and tomato paste and simmer covered for a minimum of 30 minutes.
4. Cook lasagna noodles as directed.
5. Combine ricotta cheese, Romano cheese, parsley flakes, eggs, salt and pepper in a bowl.
6. Place half the noodles in an 8 x 11 inch baking dish.
7. Spread half the cheese mixture on top then add ⅓ of the mozzarella and half the meat sauce.
8. Repeat, ending with the remaining ⅓ of mozzarella.
9. Bake for approximately 30 minutes. Let stand 10 minutes before serving.

Anna Falcon Arthurs

TAILGATE PARTY

Nicholls State University, founded in 1946, is Thibodaux's educational pride and joy. Nicholls is home to approximately 6,000 students annually and boasts over 55,000 alumni worldwide. Nicholls has the state's only 4-year culinary program offered by the Chef John Folse Culinary Institute, which further contributes to the high quality of cuisine in and around the Thibodaux community. Here is a perfect menu for cheering on the Colonels! Colonel Pride!

MENU

CHICKEN BALL, CAJUN FIRECRACKERS, GRAPE SALSA

RED ROOSTER

PULLED PORK SLIDERS WITH ABITA ROOT BEER BBQ SAUCE, APPLE JALAPENO SLAW, ALLIGATOR SAUCE PIQUANT

PECAN COOKIES, CHOCOLATE DROP COOKIES

CHICKEN BALL

Serves: 6 to 8

Can be made in advance and stored in the freezer for 1 to 2 months.

4 tablespoons sesame seeds, toasted

1 (12.5 ounce) can shredded chicken

¼ teaspoon salt

2 tablespoons mayonnaise

8 ounces cream cheese, softened

2 tablespoons chives, chopped

1 teaspoon soy sauce

1. Toast sesame seeds on stovetop or in 350 degree oven for 10 to 15 minutes. Set aside to cool.

2. Combine all other ingredients together. Form into a ball and place in freezer.

3. Once stiff, approximately 30 to 60 minutes, roll in sesame seeds.

4. Serve with crackers or fresh veggies.

Anne Rodrigue

CAJUN FIRECRACKERS

Serves: 10 to 12

Super flavorful snack to pack for any sporting event. Made with ingredients you probably have on hand.

1 ½ cups canola oil

1 (1 ounce) package dry Ranch dressing mix

2 teaspoons red pepper flakes

1 (16 ounce) box Saltine crackers

1. Mix canola oil, Ranch dressing mix and red pepper flakes in a bowl.

2. Place crackers in large Ziploc bag and pour the mix on the crackers. Can be made in 2 batches.

3. Shake several times to coat the crackers.

4. Lay on parchment paper to dry out.

5. Best if made a day before hand so that the crackers have a chance to dry.

Kathy Ledet

GRAPE SALSA

Serves: 10 to 12

1 bunch seedless green grapes, quartered

1 bunch seedless red grapes, quartered

1 pint grape tomatoes, quartered

½ to 1 purple onion, chopped

½ green bell pepper, chopped

½ yellow bell pepper, chopped

1 jalapeno chili, seeded and chopped

3 cloves garlic, finely chopped

juice of 3 limes

1 tablespoon olive oil

salt and pepper, to taste

½ bunch cilantro, chopped

1. Combine grapes, tomatoes, onion and bell peppers.
2. To make dressing, combine jalapeno, garlic, lime juice, olive oil, salt and pepper. Mix well.
3. Pour dressing over salsa and top with cilantro, mixing before serving.
4. Serve with your favorite chips or crackers.

Neely Newchurch and
Jennifer McCollum

RED ROOSTER

Serves: 24

1 fifth vodka (750 millileters)

1 quart cranberry juice

12 ounces frozen orange juice concentrate

1. Combine all ingredients and freeze.
2. Mixture will remain as a slush.

Kathleen Gros

PULLED PORK SLIDERS WITH
ABITA ROOT BEER BBQ SAUCE

Serves: 16 to 20

PORK

1 (8 to 10 pound) pork butt

¼ cup kosher salt

¼ cup coarse ground black pepper

2 tablespoons granulated garlic

½ teaspoon cayenne pepper

2 teaspoons smoked paprika

2 to 3 onions, diced

BBQ SAUCE

6 cups Abita root beer

1 ½ cups dark brown sugar

1 cup ketchup

¼ cup white wine vinegar

¼ cup red wine vinegar

6 tablespoons A-1 Steak Sauce

2 tablespoons Dijon mustard

1 teaspoon crushed red pepper flakes

4 cinnamon sticks

8 whole cloves

1. Preheat oven to 350 degrees.

2. Cut the pork butt into 4 to 5 sections.

3. Mix salt, black pepper, garlic, cayenne pepper and paprika to make a rub. Generously season pork pieces with the rub.

4. Place into a baking dish on top of the onions, cover with aluminum foil and roast in the oven for approximately 3 hours.

5. While pork is cooking, make the BBQ sauce by adding Abita root beer, dark brown sugar, ketchup, white wine vinegar, red wine vinegar, A-1 Steak Sauce, Dijon mustard and red pepper flakes to a small sauce pot and whisk until well blended.

6. Add cinnamon sticks and cloves, put on high heat until boiling, then reduce to a light simmer.

7. Simmer for approximately 30 minutes or until sauce coats the back of a metal spoon.

8. Remove the cinnamon and cloves by straining through a fine mesh strainer.

9. When the pork is done, it should shred easily using 2 forks.

10. Pour the BBQ sauce over the pork and put back into the oven for 10 to 15 minutes.

11. Serve pulled pork on a slider bun with a scoop of Apple Jalapeno Slaw (recipe follows).

Chef Ryan Gaudet

APPLE JALAPENO SLAW

Serves: 10 to 12

2 ounces sugar

¾ ounce white wine vinegar

2 cups mayonnaise

½ ounce horseradish

4 red apples, shredded

4 green apples, shredded

2 cups lemon juice

6 cups water

4 jalapenos, diced

Chef Ryan Gaudet

1. In a large mixing bowl, dissolve sugar with vinegar, stirring with a whisk.

2. Add the mayonnaise and horseradish, blend until smooth and refrigerate.

3. Using a mandolin with the fine julienne attachment, shred the apples. A good cheese grater can be used with the large hole side if no mandolin is available.

4. As each apple is shredded, place in lemon water to prevent browning. If making ahead of time, leave apples in lemon water.

5. When ready to serve, drain the apples very well by squeezing out the lemon water and place into a mixing bowl.

6. Add the jalapenos and dressing until everything is coated well; stir to combine.

7. The slaw mixture will hold well for several hours, but not overnight.

ALLIGATOR SAUCE PIQUANT

Serves: 10 to 12

Recipe can easily be doubled depending on how much alligator meat you have.

1 ¼ cups vegetable oil

1 cup flour

8 ounces onion, thinly diced

4 ounces bell pepper, thinly diced

4 ounces celery, thinly diced

6 cups chicken broth or stock

1 (29 ounce) can tomato sauce

1 (28 ounce) can whole tomatoes, drained and diced

1 to 1 ½ pound(s) fresh alligator meat, trimmed and chopped (remove as much fat, silver skin and connective tissue as possible)

16 ounces mushrooms, sliced

2 tablespoons Worcestershire sauce

2 tablespoons Cajun seasoning

¼ cup Italian seasoning

1 ½ teaspoons granulated garlic

2 teaspoons lemon juice

cooked rice

1/3 cup green onions, chopped, to garnish

1. In a large flat-bottom pot, heat oil over high heat.

2. Slowly whisk in flour to make a light brown roux.

3. When roux is ready, add onion, bell pepper and celery and cook until soft and onions are translucent.

4. Add chicken stock slowly and whisk until blended.

5. Add tomato sauce, diced whole tomatoes, alligator, mushrooms, Worcestershire sauce, Cajun seasoning, Italian seasoning, garlic and lemon juice and bring to a simmer.

6. Cook for an hour or until alligator meat is tender.

7. Serve over steamed rice. Garnish with green onions.

Chef Ryan Gaudet

PECAN COOKIES

Serves: 54 cookies

½ pound butter

½ teaspoon vanilla extract

1 cup light brown sugar

1 cup white sugar

1 egg

½ teaspoon baking soda

3 cups flour

½ teaspoon baking powder

1 cup pecans, chopped

1. Cream butter, vanilla extract, light brown sugar, white sugar and egg using a mixer.

2. Add baking soda, flour, baking powder and pecans. Mixture will be dry.

3. Form mixture into 3 rolls, approximately 8 inches long and 1 inch thick. Wrap each in wax paper, then in aluminum foil.

4. Refrigerate overnight.

5. When ready to bake, preheat oven to 350 degrees.

6. Remove from refrigerator and slice thinly.

7. Place on cookie sheet with parchment paper and bake until brown, approximately 10 to 12 minutes.

Erin Rome Barrilleaux

CHOCOLATE DROP COOKIES

Serves: 18 cookies

COOKIES

1 ½ sticks butter

1 cup sugar

1 egg

1 teaspoon vanilla extract

2 ¼ cups all-purpose flour

½ teaspoon baking soda

½ teaspoon salt

½ cup milk

2 squares unsweetened chocolate,
   melted and cooled

FROSTING

2 tablespoons butter, softened

dash of salt

3 to 4 tablespoons milk

½ teaspoon vanilla extract

2 cups powdered sugar

1 square unsweetened chocolate, melted

1. Preheat oven to 350 degrees.
2. Cream butter and sugar until light and fluffy.
3. Beat in egg and vanilla extract.
4. Combine flour, baking soda and salt and add to creamed mixture, alternating with milk.
5. Blend in chocolate.
6. Drop by rounded spoon on greased cookie sheet.
7. Bake for 12 to 15 minutes. Remove from oven and let cool before frosting.
8. Combine all frosting ingredients and frost cookies.

Erin Rome Barrilleaux

SUGARCANE

The sugarcane industry thrives in Thibodaux with an abundance of cane fields and sugar mills. Sugar farmers start harvesting cane in the beginning of October and aim to finish by Christmas Eve, weather depending. Sure signs of grinding season are the presence of numerous harvest trucks around town and the distinct smell of cane burning while the mills are running nonstop. Try these local recipes that use cane syrup or raw cane sugar as an ingredient.

CHEF BRANDON NAQUIN

HOMETOWN:

Thibodaux, Louisiana

EDUCATION AND EXPERIENCE:

Chef Brandon earned a Bachelor of Science Degree in Culinary Arts from Nicholls State University. He worked for Rouses and Zen as a Sushi Chef and at Fremin's in Thibodaux. Chef Brandon has also had the privilege of working with several Cajun Creole chefs including John Folse, Leah Chase, John Besh, Emeril Lagasse and Paul Prudhomme. Currently, Chef Brandon is the Chef and Operator of DJ's Grille in Vacherie.

"Thibodaux is situated in the heart of bayou country. We are an hour and a half away from the best of what Louisiana has to offer: from hunting and fishing the bayous to big city life of New Orleans and Baton Rouge. The small-town setting is perfect to raise a family."

FIELD OF CANE SALAD

Serves: 4

This recipe is very versatile. Add a protein and enjoy as a main course, serve pecans during cocktail hour or use vinaigrette to dress your favorite salad.

SPICED PECANS

2 tablespoons butter

1 teaspoon Cajun seasoning

1 teaspoon cinnamon

1 teaspoon nutmeg

1 teaspoon garlic powder

1 teaspoon brown sugar

1 cup pecans, halves or pieces

CANE SYRUP VINAIGRETTE

¼ cup cane syrup

1 tablespoon garlic, minced

1 tablespoon creole mustard

¼ cup balsamic vinegar

1 tablespoon Italian dressing

1 cup vegetable oil

½ cup olive oil

salt and pepper, to taste

SALAD

1 package of lettuce mix (spring, romaine, spinach, tender lettuce)

¼ cup spiced pecans

12 large strawberries, sliced

½ red onion, finely sliced

1 cup cane syrup vinaigrette

¼ cup Feta cheese

1. Preheat oven to 350 degrees.

2. To make spiced pecans, melt butter in a large sauté pan. Add all spices and cook until fragrant.

3. Turn off heat, add pecans and stir.

4. Transfer to baking sheet and place in oven to roast for 7 to 10 minutes. Watch closely to ensure they don't burn.

5. To make vinaigrette, in a large mixing bowl using a wire whisk, combine cane syrup, garlic, creole mustard, balsamic vinegar and Italian dressing.

6. Continue to whisk and slowly add vegetable oil and olive oil in a steady stream to form an emulsion. Taste and season with salt and pepper if necessary.

7. To assemble salad, in a large bowl, add lettuce, spiced pecans, strawberries and onion.

8. Toss with ½ of the vinaigrette and portion onto desired plates.

9. Drizzle remaining dressing and top with Feta cheese.

Chef Brandon Naquin

CANE SYRUP BRINE AND
SIMPLE ROAST CHICKEN

Serves: approximately 4 liters

CANE SYRUP BRINE

8 cups water

2/3 cup salt

3/4 cup cane syrup

1/2 cup brown sugar

2 teaspoons onion powder

1 tablespoon garlic powder

1 tablespoon black pepper

2 teaspoons thyme

8 cups ice

1 or 2, 5 to 6 pound chicken(s)

1. Combine all ingredients except ice and chicken in a large saucepan.

2. Heat over medium heat until the dry ingredients are dissolved.

3. Add ice to cool the brine. Once cooled to room temperature, brine is ready for use.

4. For chicken, rinse and clean 1 or 2, 5 to 6 pound chicken(s), removing neck and giblets.

5. Place chicken in cooled brine and refrigerator for 24 hours. Do not exceed 24 hours of brining, or meat may become overly dry.

6. The following day, rinse and pat dry chicken(s) and cook using your favorite method. Consider simple roast chicken as outlined on the following page.

7. This brine would also work for a 12 to 14 pound turkey, or a large amount (5 to 6 pounds) of pork such as a Boston butt, loin chops or rib chops, cooked using your favorite method.

Chef Brandon Naquin

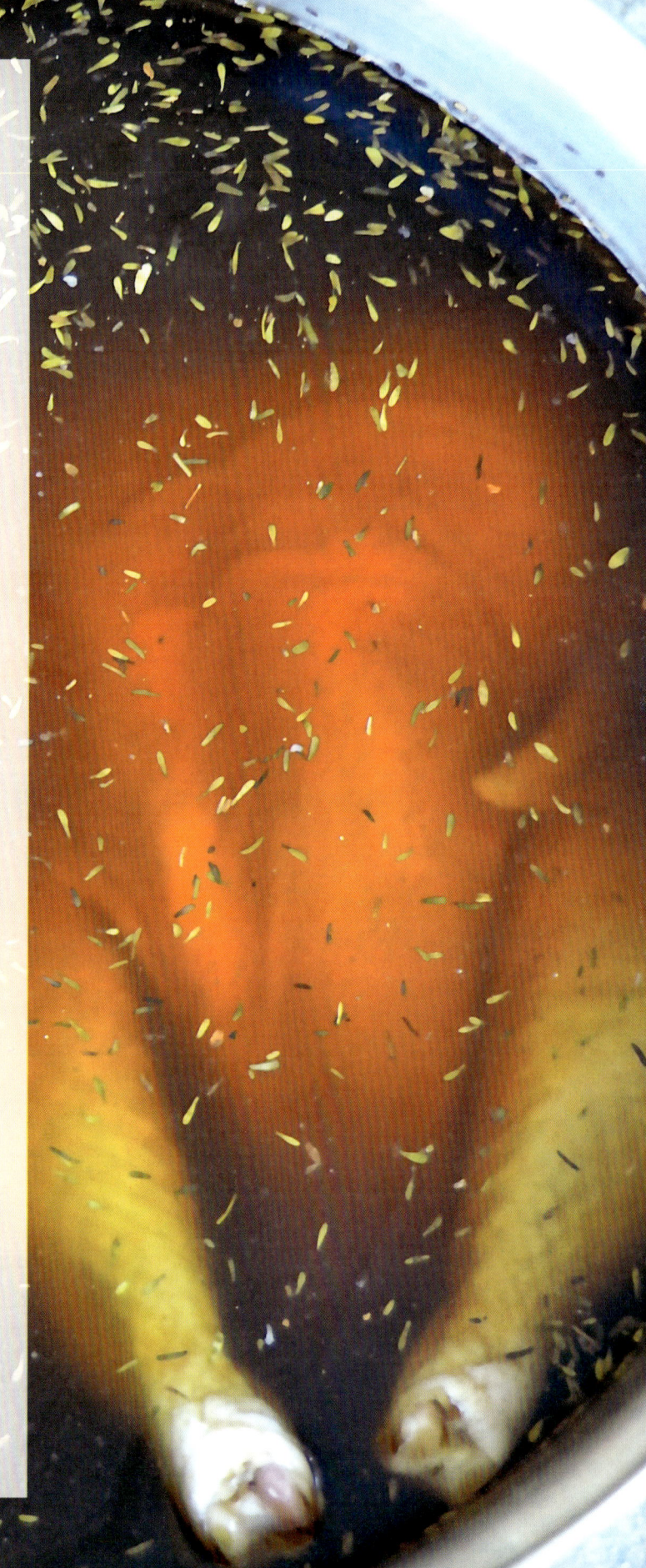

SIMPLE ROAST CHICKEN

5 to 6 pound whole
  chicken, cleaned

1 lemon, sliced

2 sprigs thyme

2 sprigs rosemary

2 tablespoons salt

2 tablespoons pepper

1. Preheat oven to 425 degrees and arrange oven racks so chicken will be positioned in the bottom third of the oven.

2. Clean chicken, removing neck and giblets, pat dry and allow to come to room temperature.

3. Stuff chicken cavity with lemon, thyme and rosemary and seal cavity by trussing chicken using kitchen twine.

4. Season generously with salt and pepper.

5. Place on a roasting pan to allow drippings to accumulate below the meat.

6. Place chicken in oven, and roast for 15 to 20 minutes until skin is browning.

7. Lower the oven temperature to 375 degrees, and roast for an additional 60 to 70 minutes, until thermometer reads 165 degrees when placed in thigh. If skin begins to look too brown at any point, can tent with aluminum foil.

8. Remove from oven and let rest 10 to 15 minutes before serving.

9. Drippings collected below can be served alongside the chicken, used to make a gravy or simply discarded.

Anne Rodrigue

RAW SUGAR CAKE

Serves: 10 to 12

4 eggs

2 cups biscuit mix

2 cups raw sugar

2 cups pecans, chopped

powdered sugar, to garnish

1. Preheat oven to 350 degrees.

2. Mix eggs, biscuit mix, sugar and pecans. Pour into a greased 13 x 9 inch pan.

3. Bake for 20 to 30 minutes.

4. Sift powdered sugar on top of cooled cake.

Marie W LeBlanc

GINGERBREAD CAKE

Serves: 10 to 12

1 cup sugar

1 cup butter, melted

2 eggs

1 teaspoon baking soda

1 teaspoon cinnamon

1 teaspoon ground cloves

1 teaspoon allspice

2 ½ cups flour

2 cups cane syrup

1 cup boiling water

1. Preheat oven to 350 degrees.
2. Mix all ingredients together in a deep bowl with a wire whisk. Consistency will be very thin.
3. Pour into greased 9 x 13 inch metal or glass pan. Recipe may be cut in half using a 9 x 9 inch pan.
4. Bake for 45 minutes.
5. Cool before cutting. Top with favorite frosting, if desired.

Brenda G Riviere

CREAM CHEESE ICING

Serves: 2 quarts

½ cup margarine or butter

1 (8 ounce) package cream cheese, softened

1 pound powdered sugar

½ teaspoon vanilla extract

1. Cream margarine, cream cheese and sugar.
2. Beat until smooth.
3. Add vanilla extract.
4. Spread on cooled cake.

Barbara "Bobbie" Fakier Harrison

FAMILY MEALS

Family meals, especially Sunday family lunches, are a tradition in South Louisiana, and Thibodaux is no exception. These dishes are perfect for small or large gatherings of family and friends when you have a little more time to enjoy cooking.

OYSTERS WITH SPINACH AND ARTICHOKES

Serves: 8

2 to 3 dozen oysters, drained (reserve liquid)

3 tablespoons butter

½ cup onion, finely chopped

¼ cup celery, finely chopped

¼ cup red bell pepper, finely chopped

4 cloves garlic, minced

¼ cup green oinons, chopped

2 pounds fresh baby spinach or 2 (8 ounce) packages of chopped frozen spinach, thawed and drained

¼ cup reserved oyster liquid

4 ounces low fat cream cheese

1 teaspoon Worcestershire sauce

1 (14 ounce) can quartered artichokes in water, drained

2 tablespoons fresh basil or oregano, chopped

salt and pepper, to taste

cayenne pepper, to taste

2 dashes hot sauce

1 cup plain breadcrumbs

½ cup Parmesan cheese, grated

2 tablespoons butter, cut into small cubes

1. Preheat oven to 350 degrees.

2. Drain oysters and reserve liquid.

3. Melt butter in large skillet, sauté onion, celery, bell pepper and garlic until vegetables are tender.

4. Add green onions and stir.

5. Add spinach and stir until wilted.

6. Add oyster liquid, cream cheese, Worcestershire sauce, artichokes and herbs.

7. Cook over medium heat, stirring well.

8. Gently stir in oysters and cook until they curl, stirring regularly.

9. Add additional oyster liquid if too thick (oysters will release liquid as they cook).

10. Add salt, pepper, cayenne pepper and hot sauce.

11. Spoon mixture into a buttered 8 x 8 inch baking dish or 6 to 8 ramekins.

12. Sprinkle with breadcrumbs, Parmesan cheese and cubes of butter.

13. Bake until bubbly and lightly brown on top, approximately 25 minutes, less for ramekins.

Betsy H Magee

MEATBALLS AND TOMATO GRAVY

Serves: 10 to 12

Sautéed chicken or boneless pork fingers can be added to gravy with meatballs. Alternatively, a peeled and cut eggplant can also be added to gravy an hour before dish is done.

TOMATO GRAVY

1 cup onions, chopped

1/4 cup bell pepper, chopped

1/4 cup olive oil

1 (14.5 ounce) can stewed tomatoes

2 (12 ounce) cans tomato paste

3 to 4 cloves garlic, chopped

Cajun seasoning, to taste

1/3 cup sugar

1 cup mushrooms, sliced (optional)

2 quarts boiling water

MEATBALLS

3 pounds ground chuck

1/3 cup onion, finely chopped

1/3 cup green onion, finely chopped

1 to 3 clove(s) garlic, finely chopped

1 egg, beaten

2/3 cup breadcrumbs

Cajun seasoning, to taste

dried parsley flakes, to garnish

cooked spaghetti

1. To make gravy, cook onions and bell pepper in olive oil until tender.

2. Add stewed tomatoes and stir.

3. Add tomato paste, stir and cook on medium heat for approximately 15 minutes.

4. Add garlic and Cajun seasoning, stir.

5. Add sugar and cook for approximately 5 minutes.

6. Add sliced mushrooms, if desired.

7. Add 2 quarts of boiling water, a little at a time, stirring to blend.

8. To make meatballs, combine ground chuck, onion, green onion (save a handful to garnish), garlic, egg, breadcrumbs and Cajun seasoning.

9. Form into medium sized meatballs.

10. Drop meatballs into gravy and cook slowly for 3 hours. Stir occasionally, making sure to not burn. Add more water if sauce becomes too thick.

11. Add a sprinkle of dried parsley flakes and green onions and serve over spaghetti.

Mary Bilello Diedrich

BAKED BRISKET

Serves: 10 to 12

Great comfort food to deliver to friends or family. Serve with white beans, rice dressing and coleslaw.

1 (10 pound) brisket

salt and pepper, to taste

Worcestershire sauce, to taste

¼ teaspoon liquid smoke

garlic salt, to taste

onion salt, to taste

seasoned salt, to taste

2 onions, chopped

2 onions, cut into rings

1 to 2 can(s) beef consommé, more if additional sauce desired

1 to 2 cup(s) red wine, more if additional sauce desired

1. Preheat oven to 400 degrees.

2. Season brisket generously with salt and pepper, Worcestershire sauce, liquid smoke, garlic salt, onion salt and seasoned salt.

3. Put seasoned brisket in a pan in which meat fits closely and pack with 2 medium chopped onions.

4. Bake in oven for 1 hour; then turn brisket over and bake for another hour. Brisket should be browned at this point.

5. Place onion rings on top and sides.

6. Add 1 can beef consommé and 1 cup red wine and cover tightly.

7. Cook for 3 to 4 hours, until tender. Check throughout baking time and if more gravy is desired add another can of consommé and 1 cup red wine.

8. Remove brisket from sauce and let rest.

9. If serving immediately, trim fat and slice meat across grain with electric knife, place slices of brisket in gravy.

10. The brisket can be cooked the day before and refrigerated whole.

11. To prepare after refrigeration, slice against grain, while cold, place cut brisket in gravy, and heat covered in oven for 30 minutes.

Jennifer Jones Rodrigue

CHEF
LINDSAY R MASON

HOMETOWN:

Thibodaux, Louisiana

EDUCATION AND EXPERIENCE:

Chef Lindsay started working in the kitchen at the age of 15 as a dishwasher at Flanagan's Creative Food and Drink. He continued to work in several facets of that restaurant before becoming the Executive Chef at Bayou Country Club. He then moved into a position as Catering Chef at Fremin's and can currently be found at Christiano Ristorante in Houma, where he is the Executive Chef.

"Thibodaux is home no matter where my travels and love of food take me. Thibodaux is where I feel just right. The people, the culture, the bayou, it all just feels simple and safe and I'll always call it home."

STEAK DIANE

Serves: 2

JACK MARINADE

1 teaspoon crushed red pepper flakes

¼ cup Jack Daniels

2 tablespoons brown sugar

½ cup cold beef stock

½ teaspoon sesame oil

1 teaspoon lemon juice

STEAK

4 to 5 ounces beef tenderloin, pounded thin

salt and pepper, to taste

½ cup seasoned flour

1 tablespoon olive pomace oil or extra virgin olive oil

¼ cup shallots, thinly shaved

1 ½ teaspoons garlic paste

1 tablespoon Dijon mustard

1 tablespoon parsley, chopped

¼ cup brandy

small splash Worcestershire sauce

½ cup demi-glace

2 tablespoons cold butter

1. Mix together all marinade ingredients.
2. Cut beef into 1 to 2 ounce pieces, pound thin, season with salt and pepper and cover in marinade for 30 minutes.
3. Remove from marinade and pat dry. Dust in seasoned flour.
4. In a sauté pan, heat oil. Add beef to pan and sauté 30 seconds and flip.
5. Add shallots and sauté 30 seconds.
6. Add garlic paste, Dijon and parsley and sauté 30 seconds.
7. Add brandy, Worcestershire sauce and demi-glace.
8. Reduce by half, on medium heat sirring constantly.
9. Turn off heat and add butter.
10. Serve immediately.

Chef Lindsay R Mason

COQ AU VIN

This recipe uses an airline chicken, which is the boneless breast meat with the wing still attached (can be ordered from a butcher ahead of time). Other cuts such as thighs or legs work equally as well or even duck and turkey can be a fun way to give this dish personal flair.

1 pound assorted pearl onions

7 airline chicken breasts

salt and pepper, to taste

¼ cup water

8 ounces thick cut bacon

8 ounces portabella mushrooms, cubed

1 cup flour

4 stalks celery, largely diced

6 cloves garlic, smashed

½ cup tomato sauce

1 ½ bottles merlot

1 tablespoon flour

1 tablespoon butter, melted

1 pound small new potatoes

1 large carrot, diced

2 large sprigs of thyme

2 bay leaves

Chef Lindsay R Mason

1. Preheat oven to 325 degrees.

2. Bring a large pot of salted water to boil. Cut off tops and bottoms of onions and cut an "X" in root side. Boil for 1 minute. Allow to cool, remove skins and set aside.

3. Dry chicken and season with salt and pepper, set aside.

4. In a large Dutch oven, heat water and bacon on high heat until the bacon is mostly cooked.

5. Add onions and mushrooms and brown. Turn off heat and remove bacon, onions and mushrooms.

6. Dredge chicken in flour and brown on medium heat in the bacon fat that remains in the pan.

7. Add celery and garlic, cooking until garlic starts to brown.

8. Add tomato sauce and allow to cook, stirring and scraping constantly until tomato sauce darkens into a dark reddish-brown color.

9. Deglaze with 2 cups red wine, scraping pan well. Add the rest of wine. Boil 5 minutes.

10. Allow to sit for a half an hour in order for flavors to soak into chicken.

11. Cover pan or transfer to a roasting pan and cover with foil. Bake in oven for 1 ½ hours.

12. Mix flour and butter in a small mixing bowl.

13. Remove chicken from oven and add potatoes, carrot, thyme, bay leaves, bacon, onion and mushroom mixture and gently stir in flour butter mixture.

14. Cover and cook an additional 1 ½ hours. Remove from oven and allow to rest 30 minutes prior to serving.

MASHED POTATOES AND TURNIPS

Serves: 10 to 12

8 potatoes, peeled and quartered

3 turnips, peeled and quartered

4 tablespoons butter

1 cup of milk

salt and pepper, to taste

1. Boil potatoes and turnips in salted water until fork tender.
2. Drain and mash, adding butter and milk. Season with salt and pepper.
3. Serve immediately.

Patrick Ellender

BRAISED SHORT RIBS

Serves: 6 to 8

Other sides that pair well with these delicious short ribs include cornbread and smothered collard greens.

6 pounds of bone-in thick cut short ribs

½ cup flour

salt and pepper, to taste

7 tablespoons olive oil, divided

3 yellow onions, chopped

4 carrots, diced

6 cloves garlic, thinly sliced

2 stalks celery, chopped

1 bottle dry red wine

2 (30 ounce) cans beef broth

4 bay leaves

2 sprigs rosemary

2 sprigs thyme

2 tablespoons cornstarch mixed with 4 tablespoons cold water, more for thicker gravy

Patrick Ellender

1. Preheat oven to 350 degrees.

2. Dust the short ribs in flour followed by salt and pepper.

3. In a large Dutch oven, add 3 tablespoons of olive oil and brown the short ribs for 2 to 3 minutes on each side. Remove the short ribs and put to the side.

4. In the same Dutch oven, add 4 tablespoons olive oil and sauté onions, carrots, garlic and celery until soft, approximately 5 to 10 minutes.

5. Remove vegetables and put to the side. Add approximately ¾ of the bottle of wine to the pot, scraping the bottom to deglaze (drink the rest).

6. Bring liquid to a boil for approximately 10 minutes, which will reduce the volume by ½ to ¾.

7. Once reduced, return short ribs and vegetables to pot.

8. Add beef broth until all the ribs are covered with liquid. If additional liquid needed, add water or additional broth.

9. Add bay leaves, rosemary and thyme and place in oven for 4 to 6 hours until rib meat is falling off bone.

10. Remove short ribs from liquid, debone and skim grease from liquid.

11. To thicken the sauce, bring to a boil and slowly add cornstarch and cold water mixture.

12. When the sauce is thickened, the chunks of short rib meat can be added back.

PAN ROASTED PORK TENDERLOIN
WITH CAPER SAUCE

Serves: 4

1 pound pork tenderloin, cleaned
   and trimmed

sea salt, to taste

cracked black pepper, to taste

2 tablespoons extra virgin olive oil

¼ cup onion, finely diced

¼ cup yellow or red bell pepper,
   finely diced

2 tablespoons shallots, diced

2 cloves garlic, minced

4 ounces vodka

2/3 cup heavy cream

2 tablespoons capers

1 ounce fresh lemon juice

1 tablespoon fresh parsley, chopped

Senator Norby Chabert

1. Preheat oven to 350 degrees.

2. Heat oven safe pan on medium high heat on the stove top.

3. Season pork with sea salt and cracked black pepper.

4. Add extra virgin olive oil to the pan and sear the seasoned tenderloin on all sides until a light golden brown crust is achieved.

5. Place pan in the oven and cook the tenderloin until an internal temperature of 150 degrees is reached, approximately 15 to 20 minutes.

6. Remove pan from oven and place on stove top over medium heat. Remove the tenderloin from the pan and set aside to rest the meat.

7. Add onion to pan and sauté for 2 minutes.

8. Add bell pepper and sauté for 2 minutes.

9. Add shallots and garlic and sauté for an additional 2 minutes.

10. Add vodka and cook until the alcohol burns off. Can flambé if desired.

11. Add heavy cream, capers, lemon juice and parsley. Bring to a simmer and reduce until sauce achieves desired thickness.

12. Slice tenderloin into medallions and drizzle sauce over the servings.

13. Serve with Brussels sprouts as side dish.

BRUSSELS SPROUTS

Serves: 4

3 tablespoons olive oil, divided

¼ cup red onion, diced

1 cup Brussels sprouts, halved

¼ cup water

1 clove garlic, diced

salt and pepper, to taste

1. Preheat a skillet on stove top over medium heat.
2. Add 2 tablespoons of olive oil and red onion, sauté for 2 minutes.
3. Add 1 cup of evenly halved Brussels sprouts and sauté for 2 to 3 minutes.
4. Add ¼ cup of water to pan, stir, then cover and cook until water evaporates away.
5. Uncover, add another tablespoon of olive oil and garlic.
6. Sauté for 2 to 3 minutes.
7. Add salt and pepper to taste.

Senator Norby Chabert

RICE CONSOMMÉ

1 medium onion, chopped

1 bell pepper, chopped

1 stick butter

1 (16 ounce) can beef consommé

1 (16 ounce) can water

1 ½ cups rice

salt and pepper, to taste

Tony Chachere's seasoning, to taste

1. Preheat oven to 350 degrees.

2. In a saucepan, sauté onion and pepper in butter until soft.

3. In greased, round baking dish, combine all other ingredients.

4. Add onion and pepper mixture.

5. Bake uncovered for 1 hour.

Melanie Delaune and Melissa Clement,
in memory of Vernice Thibodeaux

MOMMA'S STRING BEAN AND ARTICHOKE CASSEROLE

Serves: 8 to 10

This recipe can be cut in half if you like. You can prepare it the night before and cook it the next day.

4 (14.5 ounce) cans French cut string beans, drained

2 (14 ounce) cans artichoke hearts, strained and chopped

1 cup reserved artichoke juice

3 cups Italian breadcrumbs, divided

16 ounces Parmesan cheese, grated

3 teaspoons garlic, chopped

1 ½ cups olive oil plus 2 tablespoons

salt and pepper, to taste

2 lemons, 1 sliced

¼ cup margarine or butter, sliced

1. Preheat oven to 350 degrees.

2. In a large bowl, add beans, artichoke hearts, artichoke juice, 2 cups breadcrumbs, Parmesan cheese, garlic and olive oil, stirring between each addition.

3. Mix well, add salt and pepper to taste.

4. Place in a 9 x 13 inch glass casserole dish. Cover with remaining 1 cup breadcrumbs and squeeze 1 lemon on top and slice the other to garnish.

5. Place slices of margarine or butter on top. Drizzle remaining 2 tablespoons olive oil on top.

6. Bake uncovered for 30 minutes or until golden brown.

Amanda Enclade Fremin

BOURSIN POTATOES

Serves: 8 to 10

*Can top with additional grated hard cheese towards end of baking,
for extra finesse.*

3 pounds new potatoes, eyes cleaned, thinly sliced (using a mandolin can be helpful)

salt and pepper, to taste

1 package Boursin Garlic and Fine Herb Gournay Cheese

1 (16 ounce) carton heavy whipping cream

parsley or chives, chopped

1. Preheat oven to 350 degrees.
2. Place sliced potatoes in a greased 9 x 12 inch baking dish. Potatoes should be placed in the dish in rows, end to end.
3. Season each layer with salt and pepper.
4. In a small saucepan, melt Boursin Cheese in heavy whipping cream.
5. Pour this mixture over the potatoes.
6. Place in oven, baking uncovered for 45 minutes. Potatoes are finished when they begin to brown.
7. Top with a sprinkle of parsley or chives.

Anne Rodrigue

PUMPKIN CRUNCH

Serves: 12 to 15

Best when made a day ahead.

CAKE

1 (16 ounce) can pumpkin

1 (12 ounce) can pet milk

1 cup sugar

½ teaspoon cinnamon

3 eggs

1 (15.25 ounce) box yellow cake mix

1 cup pecans, chopped

2 sticks butter, melted

FROSTING

8 ounces cream cheese

1 ½ cups powdered sugar, sifted

¾ cup Cool Whip

1. Preheat oven to 350 degrees.

2. Mix pumpkin, pet milk, sugar and cinnamon and beat in eggs.

3. Butter 9 x 13 inch pan. Line with wax paper and pour in pumpkin mixture.

4. Sprinkle boxed cake mix over pumpkin mixture.

5. Spread pecans over cake and spoon melted butter over top of cake mix.

6. Bake at 350 degrees for 50 to 55 minutes and cool.

7. To make frosting, beat cream cheese and sugar and fold in Cool Whip.

8. To assemble, flip cake onto a serving platter then ice with frosting.

9. Refrigerate until ready to serve.

Stella Prosperie

MRS. LIB'S PISTACHIO MARBLE CAKE

Serves: 12

This marble cake is both beautiful and flavorful.

1 (15.25 ounce) package lemon cake mix

1 (3.4 ounce) package Jello Pistachio Instant Pudding and Pie Filling

4 eggs

1 cup water

½ cup canola oil

½ teaspoon almond extract

¼ cup chocolate syrup

confectioners sugar (optional)

1. Preheat oven to 325 degrees.

2. Combine cake mix, pudding mix, eggs, water, canola oil and almond extract in large mixing bowl. Blend; then beat at medium speed with electric mixer for 2 minutes.

3. Split batter in half and stir in chocolate syrup to 1 half.

4. Spoon alternating batters into a greased and floured 10 inch Bundt or tube pan. Zigzag spatula through batter to marble.

5. Bake for 50 minutes.

6. Cool 15 minutes; remove from pan and finish cooling on a rack.

7. Sprinkle with confectioners sugar, if desired.

Natalie Landry

CHOCOLATE CREAM PIE

Serves: 12

For a lovely presentation, cook in a clear glass dish so layers can be easily seen.

CRUST

3 egg whites, reserve yolks

1 cup sugar

12 saltine crackers, finely crumbled

½ teaspoon baking powder

½ cup pecans, chopped

1 tablespoon vanilla extract

FILLING

3 tablespoons flour

3 tablespoons cocoa

1 cup sugar

1 ½ cups milk

3 egg yolks

3 tablespoons butter

1 teaspoon vanilla extract

TOPPING

1 pint heavy whipping cream

unsweetened chocolate, to garnish

1. Preheat oven to 320 degrees.

2. Beat egg whites until stiff.

3. Slowly add sugar to egg whites until sugar is totally dissolved.

4. Add saltine crackers, baking powder, pecans and vanilla extract and mix until combined.

5. Butter a 9 inch pie plate and fill with blended "crust" mixture.

6. Bake for 30 minutes. Allow to cool. Crust will rise while baking and fall while cooling.

7. In a medium saucepan, mix flour, cocoa and sugar.

8. Slowly add milk, egg yolks and butter and cook on medium heat until thick and bubbly.

9. Remove from heat and add vanilla extract. Transfer mixture to prepared crust and allow to cool.

10. Meanwhile, beat heavy whipping cream until thickened and spread over top of cooled pie.

11. Sprinkle grated unsweetened chocolate across top.

12. Refrigerate until ready to serve.

Barbara Pierson Gauthier

CRÈME BRÛLÉE

Easy yet upscale dessert that can be made the day before serving.

1 pint half and half

1 cup whipping cream

2 tablespoons sugar

6 egg yolks, beaten

2 teaspoons vanilla extract

¾ cup light brown sugar

fresh fruit, to garnish

1. Preheat oven to 300 degrees.

2. Gently heat half and half and whipping cream in a saucepan but do not scald.

3. Add sugar and stir until dissolved.

4. Stir in egg yolks.

5. Add vanilla extract.

6. Pour into 6 to 8 individual ramekins or custard cups. Place ramekins in 9 x 13 inch backing pan. Fill pan with water.

7. Bake 60 minutes or until set.

8. Cool and chill thoroughly.

9. Reheat broiler to 350 degrees.

10. Sift brown sugar over tops of custards.

11. Set custards in pan of ice and place 6 inches below broiler. Move it around constantly to melt and not burn sugar.

12. Cool slightly and return to refrigerator to chill. May top with fresh fruit.

Brigid Grace Himel

COOLER WEATHER SALADS AND SOUPS

APPLE CRANBERRY BACON SALAD

Serves: 2 to 4

SALAD

1 (5 ounce) container of spring
   mix lettuce

¼ cup dried cranberries

¼ cup pecans, halved

2 tablespoons Feta cheese

½ cup Fuji apples, sliced

½ cup Granny Smith apples, sliced

4 slices bacon, cooked and chopped

MAPLE DIJON VINAIGRETTE

2 tablespoons extra virgin olive oil

1 tablespoon apple cider vinegar

1 ½ tablespoons maple syrup

1 ½ teaspoons Dijon mustard

salt and pepper, to taste

1. Combine all salad ingredients in a salad bowl and mix.

2. Add vinaigrette ingredients together in a mason jar, close lid and shake to combine.

3. Pour vinaigrette over salad right before serving.

Erika Grabert

SWEET GRAPE SALAD

Serves: 12 to 15

Great for a party. Served best in a trifle dish.

2 pounds seedless green grapes, sliced in half lengthwise

2 pounds seedless red grapes, sliced in half lengthwise

8 ounces sour cream

8 ounces cream cheese, softened

½ cup white sugar

1 teaspoon vanilla extract

¾ cup light brown sugar

1 cup pecans, chopped

1. Mix green and red grapes together and set aside.
2. In a separate bowl, mix sour cream, cream cheese, white sugar and vanilla extract until blended.
3. Combine mixture with grapes. Cover bowl and chill overnight.
4. For topping, combine brown sugar and pecans.
5. Sprinkle over grape mixture right before serving.

Jessica L Vicknair

HOUSE OF FASHION CHICKEN SALAD

Serves: 20 to 30

This chicken salad recipe is served at the House of Fashion for customers while they do their holiday shopping.

1 pound walnuts, shelled

4 regular rotisserie chickens

1 bunch celery, finely chopped

1 (8 ounce) jar sweet pickle relish

¾ (30 ounce) jar mayonnaise

4 tablespoons Dijon mustard

2 pounds purple seedless grapes, sliced in halves

1. Preheat oven to 350 degrees.

2. Break walnuts into small pieces and toast for approximately 20 to 30 minutes. Stir occasionally while toasting.

3. Debone chickens and chop coarsely.

4. Add celery and sweet pickle relish to chicken and mix.

5. Add mayonnaise and mustard, mix well. This can be prepared the night before.

6. Right before serving, add walnuts and grapes to chicken salad and mix well.

7. Serve on lettuce leaf.

Sheila T Boudreaux

OYSTER SOUP

Serves: 8 to 10

1 pound bacon, cubed

1 pound Cajun vegetable trinity

1 clove garlic, minced

½ gallon of oysters, cut in ½ or 1/3 if large (reserve 2 to 3 cups liquid)

1 pint heavy whipping cream

8 ounces sharp Cheddar cheese, shredded

salt and pepper, to taste

garlic powder, to taste

Louisiana Hot Sauce, to taste

Jason G Jones

1. Fry bacon in pot until crispy, being careful not to let the bacon over cook. Remove bacon from pot and place on paper towel to remove excess grease.

2. Sauté vegetable trinity and garlic in remaining bacon grease until clear and soft.

3. Add oysters and cook until curled, less than 5 minutes.

4. Add heavy cream and approximately 2 cups of oyster liquid, more or less liquid depending on desired consistency and oyster flavor.

5. Add Cheddar cheese, allow to melt, then add cooked bacon.

6. Season to taste with salt, pepper, garlic powder and Louisiana Hot Sauce.

7. Cook on low heat for 30 plus minutes then simmer until ready to serve, stirring frequently to prevent sticking.

PUMPKIN SOUP

For an impressive presentation, serve in a hollowed out gourd.

2 tablespoons butter

¼ cup onion, finely chopped

1 tablespoon flour

2 cups cooked pumpkin (may substitute canned pumpkin)

1 teaspoon brown sugar

1/8 teaspoon nutmeg

1 teaspoon salt

1/8 teaspoon pepper

3 ½ cups chicken broth

2 cups heavy cream

1. In a 4 quart heavy saucepan, melt butter.
2. Add onion and flour, sauté for 2 to 3 minutes.
3. Stir in pumpkin.
4. In a separate bowl, combine brown sugar, nutmeg, salt and pepper and add to pumpkin mixture.
5. Stir in chicken broth and bring to a simmer. Remove from heat for a few minutes to combine flavors.
6. Stir in cream and return to a simmer.
7. Adjust seasonings to taste, serve immediately.

Sarah Chauvin

FENNEL, POTATO AND LEEK SOUP

Serves: 6 to 8

3 tablespoons butter

2 heads fennel, bulbs and stalks diced
   into ¼ inch pieces

2 leeks, diced into ¼ inch pieces

4 potatoes, peeled and diced into
   ¼ inch pieces

6 cups chicken broth

2 carrots, diced

1 red pepper, diced

1 cup half and half

salt and pepper, to taste

1. Melt butter in large pot over medium heat.

2. Add fennel, cook and stir until fragrant, approximately 5 minutes.

3. Stir in leeks and cook until slightly softened, 5 to 10 minutes.

4. Add potatoes and broth.

5. Bring soup to a boil, reduce heat and simmer until vegetables are very tender, approximately 20 minutes.

6. Purée soup in blender or with an immersion blender until smooth.

7. Add carrots and red bell pepper, simmer until softened.

8. Add half and half and salt and pepper to taste.

9. Reheat to serve or can be served cold.

Jean B Ayo

WINTER

Winter time in South Louisiana is a cherished time of year. It's the season for hunting, gumbo, citrus and time to spend Thanksgiving and Christmas with family and friends.

IN SEASON

APPLES	DATES	ORANGES
BEETS	GRAPEFRUIT	RADISHES
BLACK CHERRIES	KALE	SATSUMAS
BLOOD ORANGES	LEEKS	SPINACH
CABBAGE	LEMONS	SWEET POTATOES
CARROTS		TURNIPS

SPORTSMAN'S PARADISE

Louisiana is widely known as "Sportsman's Paradise" due to its unique environment, which makes it not only great for fishing but also for hunting waterfowl, deer and other small game. Louisiana's best hunting is in November, December and January. During these months, residents often spend as much time as possible at the "hunting camp" enjoying time outdoors with family and friends and marveling at God's creation evident in the local landscape overflowing with wildlife.

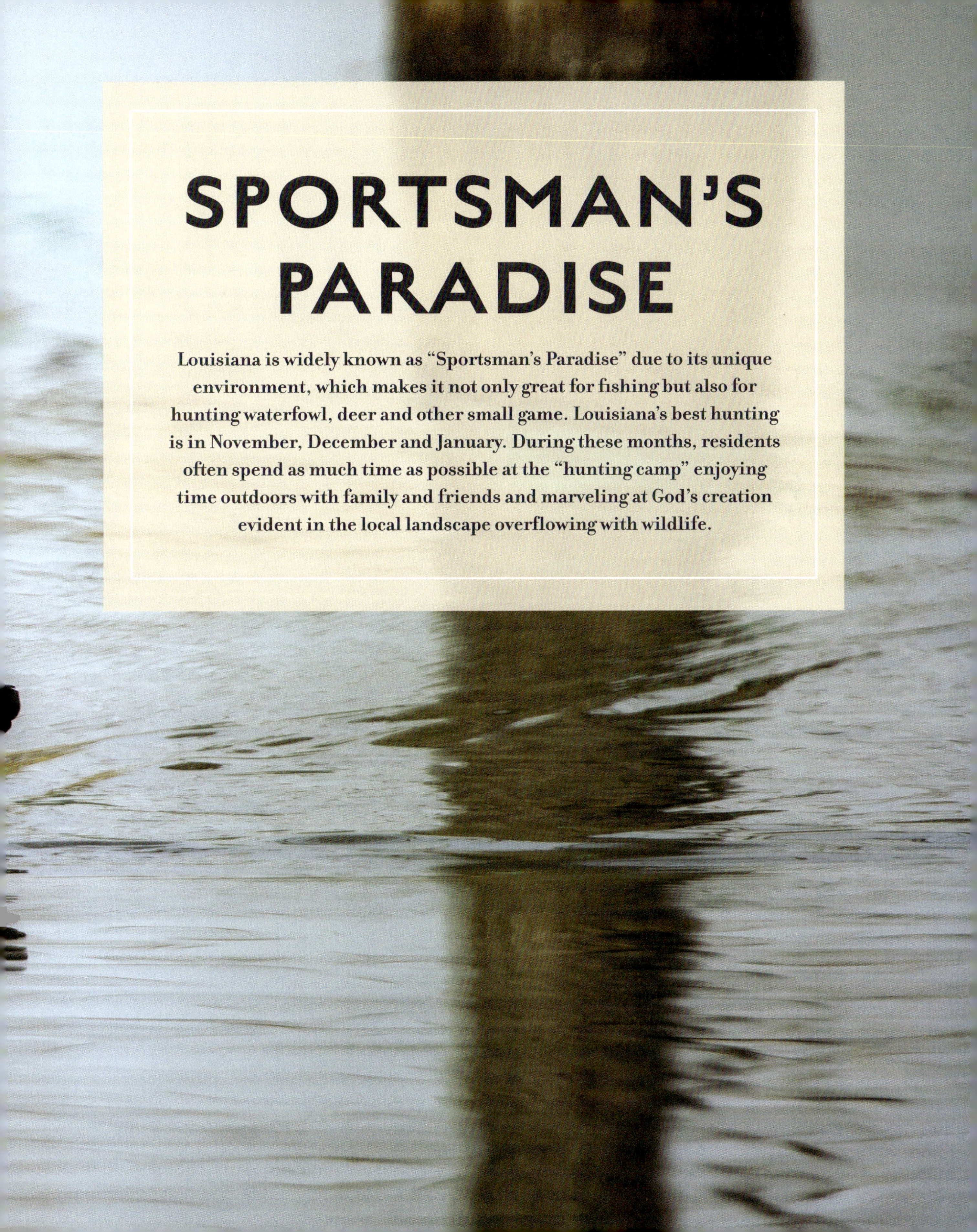

DUCK AND WAFFLES WITH ROOT BEER BOURBON GLAZE

Serves: 6

Winner of cook-off at Louisiana Ducks Unlimited State Convention.

DUCK STRIPS

1 ½ pounds duck breast, cut into strips

salt and pepper, to taste

½ cup of flour

2 eggs, whisked

1 ½ cups panko breadcrumbs

1 ½ cups pecans, chopped

½ teaspoon cayenne pepper

frying oil

GLAZE

2 (12 ounce) cans root beer

3 tablespoons red hot pepper jelly

2 tablespoons steak sauce

2 tablespoons orange juice

1 ½ cups bourbon

1 cup sugar

2 teaspoons cinnamon

WAFFLES

1 (12.5 ounce) box of Zatarain's Honey Butter Cornbread Mix

½ cup milk

6 tablespoons butter, melted

1 egg

butter, to garnish

1. Season duck strips with salt and pepper.

2. For breading, set up 3 large shallow dishes. Put flour in first dish. Place whisked eggs in second dish. Combine panko, pecans and cayenne pepper and place in third dish.

3. Dredge duck strips in flour, then eggs, then coat with panko pecan mixture.

4. Deep fry duck strips.

5. To make glaze, whisk all ingredients together over medium high heat.

6. Bring mixture to a boil, whisking constantly to dissolve sugar.

7. Once mixture is boiling, reduce heat to medium and allow mixture to thicken to glaze consistency, approximately 25 to 30 minutes.

8. To prepare waffles, combine boxed cornbread mix, milk, butter and egg in a large bowl just until moistened.

9. Ladle mixture onto a greased waffle iron and cook for approximately 5 minutes. Butter waffles while hot.

10. Serve waffles topped with duck strips and drizzled with glaze.

Courtney Lichenstein

"CANARD MAGNIFIQUE"
GRILLED WILD DUCK WITH DRESSING

Serves: 10 to 12

Recipe requires 24 hours for marinade prior to cooking. For best flavor, use charcoal grill. This recipe was a Bayou Gourmet Award Winning Recipe.

MARINADE AND DUCK

6 deboned duck breasts (12 pieces)

½ cup Italian dressing

2 tablespoons White Wine Worcestershire sauce

1 to 2 teaspoon(s) Cajun seasoning

½ cup milk

salt, to taste

12 slices bacon

DRESSING

6 duck gizzards

2 quarts water

1 onion, chopped

3 tablespoons oil

1 pound ground beef

1 pound bulk pork sausage

1 cup green onions, chopped

1 cup bell pepper, chopped

1 cup celery, chopped

3 cloves garlic, minced

1 to 2 tablespoon(s) Cajun seasoning

3 cups uncooked rice

1. Pound duck breasts with meat tenderizer until thin.

2. Make marinade by combining Italian dressing, Worcestershire sauce, Cajun seasoning, milk and salt in a dish.

3. Add duck. Cover and refrigerate for 24 hours.

4. For dressing, boil gizzards in 2 quarts of water until tender, approximately 30 to 45 minutes.

5. Remove gizzards, saving the broth, and chop in a food processor.

6. In Dutch oven, brown onion in approximately 3 tablespoons of oil until caramelized and dark.

7. Add ground beef and pork sausage. Stir until brown.

8. Add gizzards, green onions, bell pepper, celery, garlic and Cajun seasoning. Sauté for 5 minutes.

9. Add 6 cups of gizzard broth, use additional water if needed.

10. Cover and cook on low for 45 minutes.

11. Raise heat and bring to a full boil. Add uncooked rice and more salt and Cajun seasoning, if needed.

12. Reduce to very low heat. Stir frequently until rice is tender and water disappears, approximately 30 minutes.

13. Preheat grill to medium heat.

14. Remove duck breast from refrigerator and wrap each piece in 1 slice of bacon. Secure with toothpick.

15. Place on grill, turning often until tender, 20 to 30 minutes.

16. Serve with duck gizzard dressing.

Janelle Bonvillain

TAT'S DUCKS

Serves: 12

You can follow the same recipe to cook duck hearts and gizzards.

vegetable oil

12 ducks with skin, cleaned and washed
(all same type of duck to cook evenly)

1 pound bacon, rendered grease

Tony Chachere's seasoning, to taste

salt and pepper, to taste

2 Red Delicious apples, cut into 6 wedges

12 cloves garlic

4 small onions, peeled and quartered

12 cups chicken broth

8 cups beef broth, divided

8 ounces fresh, wild or
Portobello mushrooms, thinly sliced

1 bunch fresh parsley, chopped

1 bunch green onions, chopped

1 to 2 tablespoon(s) Kitchen Bouquet

1 to 2 cup(s) wine or sherry (optional)

cooked wild or pecan rice

Thomas A Thomassie, III

1. In frying pan, add ¼ inch vegetable oil and heat on high.

2. Brown ducks, 2 to 3 at a time, keeping the oil hot.

3. Simultaneously, in a separate pot, large enough to fit all ducks in 1 layer, fry bacon, cooking slowly, careful not to burn. After bacon is done, remove bacon from pot and turn off heat.

4. After browning, season ducks, 1 at a time, inside and out, with Tony Chachere's seasoning, salt and pepper.

5. Stuff each duck with apple wedge, garlic clove and onion quarter.

6. Reheat bacon grease on low, scraping bottom to loosen pieces. Place ducks in pot, breast down.

7. Raise heat to medium high and brown ducks a second time until the skin is crispy.

8. Add chicken broth and 4 cups of the beef broth. Liquid should completely cover the ducks. Add more liquid if needed.

9. Carefully scrape the bottom of the pot again, keeping ducks in 1 layer, breast down.

10. Add mushrooms and cook ducks until tender, approximately 2 to 4 hours depending on type and size of duck used.

11. Once ducks are tender, remove them from the pot and reduce the liquid.

12. Add parsley, green onions and Kitchen Bouquet.

13. Once sauce is reduced, add 4 cups of beef broth and wine or sherry, if desired, to deglaze the pot and cook until sauce is thick.

14. Serve over wild or pecan rice.

SMOTHERED RABBIT

Serves: 4 to 6

Feel free to add potatoes and carrots to gravy while cooking.

1 rabbit, if wild, marinate overnight in Italian dressing

Cajun seasoning, to taste

garlic powder, to taste

onion powder, to taste

1 to 2 tablespoon(s) olive oil

Worcestershire sauce, to taste

1 large onion, chopped

16 ounces water

1 (0.87 ounce) envelope brown gravy mix

cooked rice

1. Season rabbit with Cajun seasoning, garlic powder and onion powder.

2. Brown both sides of the rabbit in olive oil, splashing with Worcestershire sauce.

3. Add onion and "smother" until onions are wilted.

4. Add water, approximately 16 ounces, to 2/3 way covering the rabbit. Stir in gravy mix and season to taste.

5. Cook for approximately 1 to 1 ½ hours on medium heat until the meat is tender. Keep adding water as needed as it cooks down.

6. Serve over hot rice.

Donna Waguespack

GRILLED VENISON BACKSTRAP WITH BLUE CHEESE SAUCE

Serves: 4 to 6

A simple and upscale preparation of venison that is very flavorful.

1 medium (approximately 2 pound) venison backstrap

salt and pepper, to taste

2 tablespoons garlic, finely chopped

1 stick butter

¼ cup extra virgin olive oil

¼ cup green onions, finely chopped

¼ cup parsley, finely chopped

6 ounces blue cheese, crumbled

1. Season backstrap generously with salt and pepper.
2. Grill backstrap to medium rare, approximately 140 degrees using a meat thermometer. Let meat rest for 10 minutes before slicing.
3. Slice backstrap into very thin pieces.
4. To make sauce, sauté garlic in butter and oil until garlic is lightly brown.
5. Add green onions and parsley and sauté until wilted.
6. Remove mixture from heat and let sit for 5 minutes, then stir in blue cheese.
7. Spoon sauce over sliced backstrap pieces.

Jane Zeringue

VENISON
BACKSTRAP PARMIGIANA

Serves: 6

For when your freezer is full of venison but you are craving Italian.

2 pounds venison backstrap, cut into ½ inch slices

2 eggs

2 tablespoons water

2 cups Italian breadcrumbs

1 cup Parmigiano-Reggiano cheese, grated

½ cup seasoned flour

½ cup vegetable oil

1 quart favorite pasta sauce

2 cups Mozzarella cheese, shredded

2 tablespoons Italian parsley, chopped

1. Preheat oven to 350 degrees.
2. Lightly pound backstrap slices to ¼ inch thickness.
3. In a shallow bowl, beat together egg and water.
4. In a separate bowl, combine breadcrumbs and 4 tablespoons Parmigiano-Reggiano cheese.
5. Dip backstrap in seasoned flour, then egg mixture and finally coat with breading mixture.
6. In a large skillet, fry breaded backstrap in oil, browning on both sides.
7. Coat the bottom of a greased 9 x 13 inch baking dish with pasta sauce.
8. Place the backstrap into the coated pan with the edges slightly overlapping. Spoon additional pasta sauce over the center of the layered backstrap.
9. Sprinkle shredded Mozzarella and remaining grated Parmigiano-Reggiano over backstrap.
10. Bake in oven for 25 to 35 minutes or until cheese is melted and sauce begins to bubble.
11. Remove from oven and sprinkle with additional Parmigiano-Reggiano and chopped parsley.

Demian Barrancotto

SHERRIED VENISON

Serves: 4 to 6

*You may substitute stew meat, 7 steaks, round steak or any other
reasonably tender cut of venison for backstrap.*

1 whole backstrap (1 side), cut into ½ to
  ¾ inch pieces

2 tablespoons all-purpose seasoning

1 cup all-purpose flour

1 to 1 ½ cup(s) butter, divided

1 bell pepper, chopped

1 bunch green onions, chopped

4 cloves garlic, minced

1 (10 ounce) can Rotel

2 (14 ounce) cans chicken broth

1 cup cooking sherry

2 tablespoons corn starch (optional)

2 ounces cool water (optional)

cooked rice

1. Slice backstrap, pat dry, season with all-purpose seasoning and coat with flour.

2. Brown venison in ½ to 1 cup butter, depending on size of backstrap, over medium to medium high heat for 15 to 20 minutes and set aside.

3. In a separate pot melt ½ cup of butter over medium heat.

4. Sauté bell pepper, green onions and garlic until soft.

5. Add venison, Rotel and chicken broth and simmer over medium heat for 1 hour. Stir often throughout the process.

6. Add sherry and simmer an additional ½ hour, stirring often.

7. If desired, you can thicken gravy by adding 2 tablespoons of corn starch to 2 ounces of cool water and slowly stir into sherried venison.

8. Serve over hot rice.

Holland Pitre

CAMP POTATOES

Serves: 6 to 8

2 tablespoons cooking oil

1 pound smoked sausage, sliced

1 medium onion, diced

1 green bell pepper, diced

1 stalk celery, diced

4 pounds of red potatoes, skin on, cubed

1 can of beer (12 ounces of chicken stock if you aren't at the camp)

1 tablespoon salt

1 (8 ounce) block Velveeta cheese, cubed

1 (6 ounce) carton sour cream

black pepper, to taste

cayenne pepper, to taste

Louisiana Hot Sauce, to taste

green onions, to garnish

1. In a Dutch oven heat cooking oil to medium heat and sauté the sausage until browned.
2. Add onion, bell pepper and celery, sauté until soft and translucent.
3. Dump in the cubed potatoes and beer (or chicken stock), add salt.
4. Cover the pot and bring to a boil.
5. Stir occasionally until potatoes are fork tender, 10 to 15 minutes.
6. Add Velveeta cheese and half the container of sour cream.
7. Add black pepper, cayenne pepper, Louisiana Hot Sauce and additional salt to taste.
8. Mash to incorporate until desired consistency is reached.
9. Garnish with additional sour cream and green onions.

Benjamin Caillouet

DEER ROAST WITH GRAVY

Serves: 4 to 6

3 to 4 pound deer roast

8 to 10 cloves garlic

salt and pepper, to taste

2 teaspoons Louisiana Hot Sauce

2 teaspoons season-all

4 tablespoons Worcestershire sauce, divided

1 cup Italian salad dressing

2 tablespoons canola oil

2 large onions, chopped

½ cup celery, chopped

½ medium bell pepper, chopped

1 to 2 cup(s) water

1. Wash roast thoroughly, stuff with several garlic cloves and season with salt, pepper, Hot Sauce, season-all and 2 tablespoons Worcestershire sauce.
2. Marinate in Italian salad dressing overnight.
3. In a large pot, add canola oil. Over medium heat sauté onions, celery and bell pepper approximately 10 minutes.
4. Add roast and brown.
5. Add water often to prevent burning and 2 tablespoons of Worcestershire sauce to make gravy.
6. Cook approximately 2 hours or until tender.

Gail Sonier

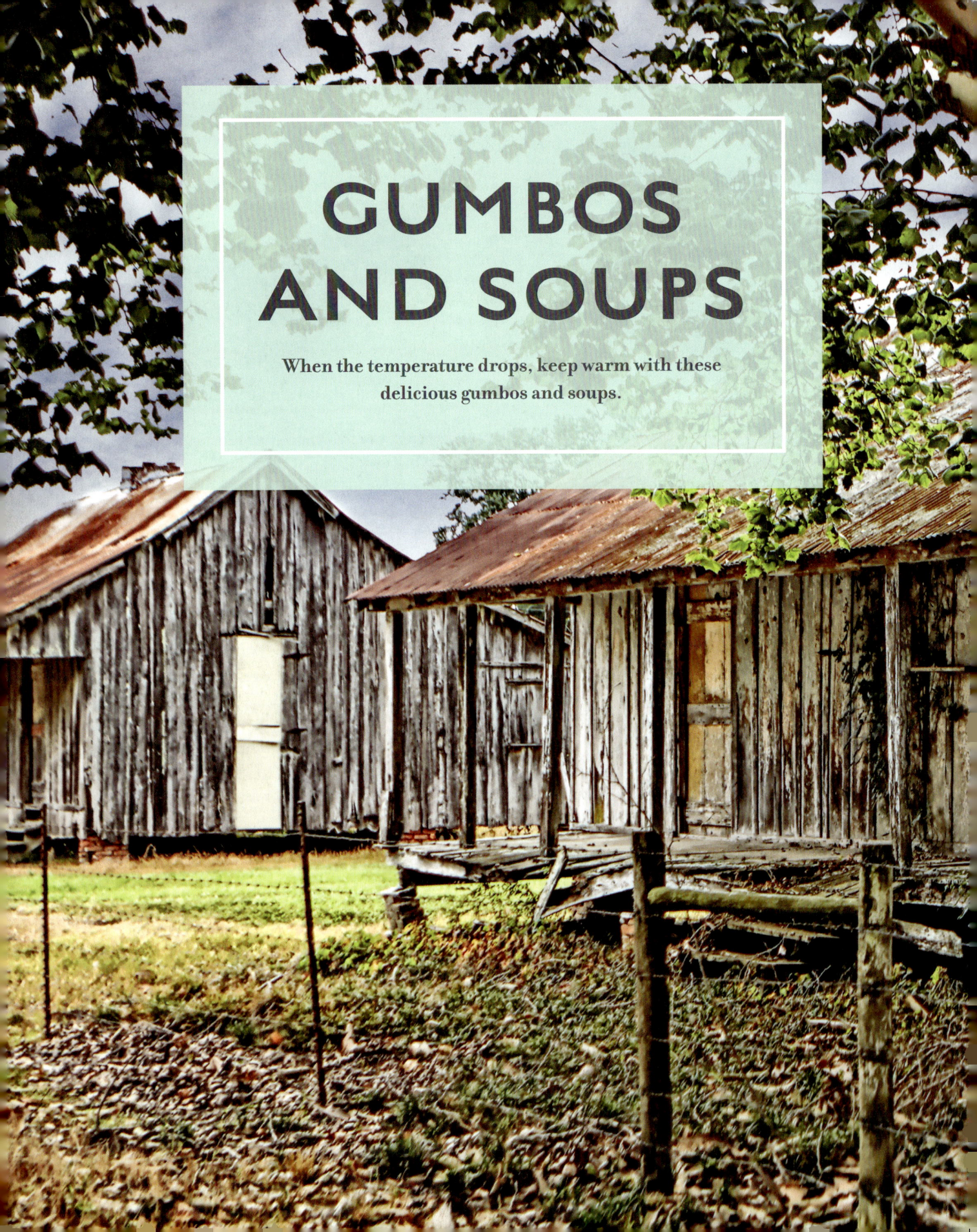

GUMBOS AND SOUPS

When the temperature drops, keep warm with these delicious gumbos and soups.

CHICKEN AND SAUSAGE GUMBO

Serves: 8 to 12

*Cold water will shock the gumbo and enhance the flavors. Many Cajuns
use a similar technique by adding ice at the end of a crawfish boil.*

1 cup vegetable oil

1 cup all-purpose flour

1 yellow onion, chopped

1 green bell pepper, chopped

3 stalks celery, chopped

2 pounds smoked sausage, sliced

2 (32 ounce) containers chicken stock

1 tablespoon Cajun seasoning

1 teaspoon salt

1 teaspoon garlic powder

3 bay leaves

2 whole rotisserie chickens, deboned

4 cups water

¼ teaspoon cayenne

1 (16 ounce) cold bottle of water

1. Make a roux by combining oil and flour over medium heat.

2. Stir regularly for roughly an hour until the roux starts to look like melted milk chocolate. For a darker roux, cook longer.

3. Add onion, bell pepper and celery and cook for another 10 minutes, stirring regularly.

4. While the vegetables are cooking, brown sausage in a separate pan. Once sausage has browned a little, add some of the chicken stock to deglaze the pan and scrape to loosen the drippings from the sausage.

5. Add the sausage and deglazed mixture to the roux and vegetable mixture and cook.

6. Add remaining chicken stock, Cajun seasoning, salt, garlic powder and bay leaves and cook for approximately 20 minutes.

7. Add chicken and 4 cups of water.

8. Bring to a boil and skim the oil off the top, if desired.

9. Simmer for 1 to 2 hours on low, stirring approximately every 15 minutes.

10. After 2 hours, add the cold water.

Jason Derouen, The Cajun Ninja

SMOKED TURDUCKEN GUMBO

Serves: 16 to 20

This gumbo won Big Boy Cook-off in 2017.

3 pounds boneless white or dark chicken

3 pounds boneless turkey breasts or thighs

4 boneless duck breasts, skin removed and reserved

5 pounds smoked sausage, cut into bite-sized pieces

2 pounds Conecuh sausage, cut into bite-sized pieces

5 pounds Cajun vegetable trinity, chopped

3 tablespoons garlic, chopped

½ bunch parsley, chopped

4 quarts water

4 quarts chicken stock

1 pound bacon

½ cup oil

1 cup flour

1 cup okra, pureed in a food processor with a small amount of water

2 (3.5 ounce) packs Mam Papaul's Gumbo mix

Kitchen Bouquet

salt and pepper, to taste

cooked rice

1. Smoke chicken, turkey and duck breasts for approximately 30 minutes in a smoker at 250 degrees. Smoke to add flavor to the meat; do not fully cook to avoid drying out.

2. Once chicken, turkey and duck have been smoked and cooled, cut into bite-sized pieces.

3. In a large pot, brown the sausages, vegetable mix, garlic and parsley.

4. After cooking down, begin to add water and stock in increments and continue to simmer.

5. Add chopped and smoked chicken, turkey and duck pieces and continue to simmer.

6. In a separate small skillet, cook bacon and duck skin until crispy. Remove bacon and duck skin from grease and let cool. (Snack on the duck and bacon crumbles as you cook.)

7. Add oil to warm duck and bacon grease to begin to make the roux. Add flour and continue to stir until the proper consistency and color of peanut butter.

8. Remove roux from heat and allow to cool.

9. Add okra to the simmering pot and cook.

10. Add Mam Papaul's gumbo mix slowly to avoid lumps.

11. After all is mixed well and simmering, slowly add roux until it is to the thickness of your liking.

12. Add Kitchen Bouquet to darken and add flavor.

13. Add salt and pepper to taste.

14. Serve over hot rice.

Tony Tranchina, Brance Lloyd and Lance Trotti

GUMBO Z'HERBES

Superstition says to use an odd number of greens. It is also says that for every number of greens you put in the pot, you will receive that many new friends within the year. The cooked greens and their broth can be made in advance and refrigerated for up to 5 days before you make the gumbo.

3 pounds greens (combination of mustard greens, collards, turnip greens, beet greens, spinach, cabbage, Brussels sprouts, radish leaves, watercress, kale, parsley and/or others), washed, tough stems removed and chopped into 1 inch pieces

3 smoked ham hocks

1 pound andouille sausage, coarsely chopped

8 cups homemade or no salt added store bought vegetable broth

water, as needed

½ cup vegetable oil

½ cup flour

1 large onion, finely chopped

1 medium green bell pepper, seeded and finely chopped

1 medium red bell pepper, seeded and finely chopped

3 stalks celery, finely chopped

6 cloves garlic, finely chopped

1 teaspoon ground cayenne pepper

2 teaspoons Cajun seasoning

2 teaspoons fine sea salt

1 teaspoon freshly ground black pepper

cooked white or brown rice

scallion tops, coarsely chopped, to garnish

1. Place greens, hocks and andouille sausage in a large pot.
2. Pour in broth, adding additional water to cover.
3. Bring to a boil over high heat, then reduce to medium or medium low heat so liquid is barely bubbling.
4. Cook greens until very tender, approximately 40 minutes. Remove from heat. Can refrigerate at this point.
5. While greens are cooking, make a roux.
6. In a separate, heavy pot, heat oil over medium heat. Once the oil shimmers, whisk in flour until smooth.
7. Reduce heat to medium low and cook, stirring constantly, until mixture turns a light brown color, 10 to 20 minutes.
8. Stir in onion, green and red bell peppers, celery, garlic, cayenne pepper, Cajun seasoning, salt and pepper.
9. Cover and cook, stirring occasionally, until the vegetables are very tender, approximately 20 minutes.
10. Drain the cooked greens, reserving the liquid. Remove the hocks.
11. Optionally, you can puree the greens for a smoother consistency.
12. Transfer the greens to the pot of vegetables. Measure out 8 cups of reserved cooking liquid and add to pot.
13. Increase heat to bring to a boil, then reduce until the liquid is barely bubbling.
14. Cook for 10 minutes to incorporate all the flavors.
15. Taste and add salt and pepper as needed.
16. Serve over hot rice and garnish with scallions.

Chef Brandon Naquin

CHEF ALZINA TOUPS

HOMETOWN:

Galliano, Louisiana

EDUCATION AND EXPERIENCE:

Alzina was born into a family of cooks and grew up living on the land and cooking with the seasons. Her restaurant, Alzina's Kitchen, was opened in 1977 in Galliano to serve St. Joseph Catholic Church for their deanery meetings. Today, Alzina's Kitchen allows only one private party at the restaurant at a time where customers eat family-style in the same room as the kitchen.

"I believe where there is good food, there's much fun. So this is why there's always finger 'lickin, pickin and tastin,' when my friends, family and grandchildren come to visit."

ROUX-LESS OKRA SEAFOOD GUMBO

Serves: 12 to 14

Down in Galliano, Louisiana, in an old welding shop on Bayou Lafourche, you can find Alzina's Restaurant. More of a "get together" place than a traditional restaurant, Alzina entertains a single dinner party at a time for a home-cooked, serve yourself meal.

2 to 3 pounds okra, fresh or frozen, tops cut off, cut into ¼ inch slices

1 to 2 tablespoon(s) vegetable oil

1 onion, chopped

½ bell pepper, chopped

1 stalk celery, chopped

1 large tomato, peeled, seeded and chopped

2 to 3 pounds shrimp, cleaned and peeled

1 to 2 pound(s) crab claws

3 bay leaves

2 to 3 quarts crab, shrimp or seafood stock (see Appendix)

salt and pepper, to taste

Tabasco sauce, to taste

Worcestershire sauce, to taste

1 (14.5 ounce) can diced tomatoes (optional)

cooked rice

1. Preheat oven to 350 degrees.
2. To make the "roux", put okra in a 3 to 4 inch high pan and mix with vegetable oil. Bake for approximately 1 ½ hours, stirring only 2 or 3 times.
3. After you take the pan out of the oven, cover it with foil so the okra does not get slimy.
4. In a gumbo pot, combine cooked okra, onion, bell pepper and celery, sauté until soft.
5. Add tomato pulp and cook into a paste.
6. Add shrimp, crab claws and bay leaves and cook for 15 minutes.
7. Add strained stock and simmer for 1 hour.
8. Season with salt, pepper, Tabasco and Worcestershire sauce to taste.
9. If gumbo is slimy from the okra, you can add a can of diced tomatoes.
10. Serve over hot rice.

Chef Alzina Toups

TATEEN'S CHICKEN ANDOUILLE OYSTER GUMBO

Serves: 12 to 14

Tateen rarely serves gumbo the day it is made. She has found that the flavors blend much better when allowed to have a day in the refrigerator. This recipe freezes well for several months.

1 small whole chicken

1 gallon water

1 pound andouille, cut into
  4 to 6 inch pieces

1 pound smoked pork sausage, cut into
  4 to 6 inch pieces

1 ½ cups flour

1 cup vegetable oil

1 cup onion, finely chopped

1 quart water

1 (14.5 ounce) can chicken broth

3 shallots, finely chopped

1 to 2 tablespoon(s) parsley, chopped

1 to 2 pint(s) oysters, drained,
  liquid reserved

salt and pepper, to taste

cooked rice

gumbo file' (optional)

1. In a large pot, cover chicken with water and boil until almost cooked.

2. Remove from boiling pot, cool, remove skin and debone.

3. Set chicken aside. Reserve stock. If stock is less than 1 gallon, add water to equal 1 gallon.

4. Gently boil andouille in stock for 30 minutes. Add smoked sausage and boil for 15 minutes.

5. Remove andouille and smoked sausage and set aside. Reserve stock.

6. In a large, heavy pot, make roux with flour and oil.

7. When roux is dark brown, add onion and cook until translucent, stirring often. Then gradually add 1 quart water, reserved stock and chicken broth.

8. Bring to a boil. Stir to mix thoroughly and reduce heat to simmer. Cover and cook for 45 minutes.

9. Meanwhile, cut cooled chicken, andouille and smoked sausage into bite sized pieces.

10. At the end of 45 minutes of cooking, add chicken and cook for additional 15 minutes.

11. Skim the oil off the top of gumbo. Then add andouille, smoked sausage, shallots and parsley.

12. Cook an additional 15 minutes. Oyster liquid can be added to taste.

13. Drop oysters in right before serving. If freezing gumbo, don't add oysters until thawed and reheated.

14. Add salt and pepper to taste.

15. Serve over steamed rice, quinoa or cauliflower rice.

16. Sprinkle with file', if desired.

Tateen Ory
Revised from original recipe in
1982 Louisiana Legacy Cookbook

SWEET POTATO AND ANDOUILLE BISQUE

Serves: 6 to 8

5 to 6 large sweet potatoes

1 pound andouille sausage, sliced and cubed

1 onion, chopped

1 red bell pepper, chopped

½ cup butter

24 ounces chicken broth

1 pint whipping cream

1 ½ teaspoons salt

¼ teaspoon black pepper

¼ teaspoon cayenne pepper

½ teaspoon nutmeg

1. Preheat oven to 400 degrees.

2. Poke several holes with fork into sweet potatoes then bake for 1 ½ to 2 hours until soft. Remove and let cool.

3. Once cooled, remove skin by hand peeling.

4. Slice andouille into 1 inch thick pieces, then cube into fourths.

5. In a large Dutch oven, over medium heat, brown andouille until edges are slightly golden. Remove andouille sausage and set aside.

6. In the same Dutch oven, sauté onion and bell pepper in butter over medium heat until tender.

7. Add sweet potatoes and chicken broth to Dutch oven, stir to combine.

8. Puree in a blender or with an immersion blender.

9. Return to Dutch oven and slowly mix in whipping cream.

10. Add andouille, salt, pepper and nutmeg and cook for another 15 minutes to incorporate flavors.

11. Serve with hot French bread or crostini.

Jeanne Glaser Higgins

SPICY CORN AND SHRIMP CHOWDER

Serves: 12

2 tablespoons butter

1 onion, chopped

½ cup shallots, chopped

½ teaspoon cumin

3 cups chicken broth

2 tablespoons cornstarch

2 cups corn, frozen or canned

1 large bell pepper, chopped

¾ cup mild salsa

2 pounds shrimp, peeled

2 cups half and half

1 pound Mexican or Jalapeno
   Velveeta cheese

1. In a pan, sauté the butter with onion, shallots and cumin.
2. Mix chicken broth with cornstarch and add to the pan.
3. Add corn, bell pepper and salsa and cook for 10 minutes.
4. Add shrimp and cook 6 additional minutes.
5. Add half and half, bring to boil, then add cheese.
6. Stir until completely melted and smooth.

Melanie Delaune and Melissa
Clement, in memory of Eldon
"Plucker" Clement

CARROT AND GINGER SOUP

Serves: 8 to 10

2 tablespoons sweet cream butter

2 onions, chopped

6 cups chicken broth

2 pounds carrots, peeled and sliced

2 tablespoons fresh ginger, grated

1 cup whipping cream

salt, to taste

white pepper, to taste

sour cream, to garnish

parsley sprigs, to garnish

1. In a sauté pan, over medium high heat, add butter and onions and cook, stirring often, until onions are soft.

2. Add broth, carrots and ginger. Cover and bring to a boil.

3. Reduce heat and simmer until carrots are fork tender, approximately 20 minutes.

4. Remove from heat and allow to cool.

5. Puree mixture using blender or immersion blender until smooth. Return to the pan and add cream.

6. Stir over high heat and bring soup to a boil.

7. Add salt and white pepper, to taste.

8. Garnish with a dollop of sour cream and parsley sprigs.

Catherine Morvant

CITRUS

Southern Louisiana's unique climate allows us to grow citrus and tropical fruits, such as kumquats, satsumas, navel oranges, grapefruit and lemons. Try these Louisiana citrus recipes when your trees ripen this winter!

SATSUMA PEPPER JELLY

Serves: 16 (4 ounce) jars

*Great as a holiday gift. Delicious when served over
cream cheese with crackers.*

1 (1.75 ounce) box Sure-Jell pectin

4 cups fresh satsuma juice

¼ cup apple cider vinegar

2 tablespoons crushed red pepper flakes

¼ teaspoon butter

7 cups sugar

16 (4 ounce) canning jars, sterilized

1. Mix pectin, satsuma juice, vinegar, pepper flakes and butter in large pot, bring to a boil that cannot be stirred down.

2. Add sugar.

3. Return to a boil that cannot be stirred down, boil 2 minutes.

4. Remove from heat, ladle into sterilized jars, put lids and rings on jars, just tighten, process in water bath for 5 minutes.

5. Remove from water bath, cool and store in cool dry place.

6. Flip jars over every 30 to 45 minutes until set to evenly disperse pepper flakes, may still rise to the top.

7. Good for 1 year.

Sarah Timberlake

BABY KALE AND LOUISIANA
CITRUS SALAD

Serves: 4 to 6

DRESSING

3 tablespoons fresh orange or satsuma juice

2 tablespoons white wine vinegar

2 ½ teaspoons Dijon mustard

1 teaspoon sugar

1 teaspoon kosher salt

1 teaspoon honey

½ teaspoon freshly ground black pepper

½ cup extra virgin olive oil

SALAD

3 large oranges

2 red grapefruits

6 to 8 ounces baby kale (or other leafy green)

½ cup red onion, thinly sliced

salt and pepper, to taste

3 ounces goat or Feta cheese, crumbled

1. To make the dressing, which can be made ahead, whisk juice, vinegar, mustard, sugar, salt, honey and pepper together.

2. Slowly drizzle in olive oil, continuously whisking, until smooth.

3. To prepare salad, peel the citrus and cut away the bitter white membrane. Place the peeled citrus in your palm, slicing between the membrane and remove whole segments.

4. Toss kale, onion and half of dressing together.

5. Add salt, pepper and/or additional dressing as needed.

6. Top with citrus and cheese and serve.

Christopher and Anne Rodrigue

BAKED SWEET POTATOES AND APPLES

Serves: 6 to 8

3 medium sweet potatoes, peeled and cut into 1 inch cubes

2 tablespoons olive oil

2 large apples, peeled and cubed (firm, sweet/tart apples such as Pink Lady)

¾ cup fresh squeezed satsuma juice (orange juice can be substituted)

¾ teaspoon cinnamon

1. Preheat oven to 400 degrees.

2. Roast diced sweet potatoes on a baking sheet with olive oil for approximately 20 minutes, or until fork tender.

3. Place roasted sweet potatoes, apples and satsuma juice in a buttered baking dish. Sprinkle with cinnamon and stir to coat apples with liquid.

4. Bake uncovered for 20 minutes or until the sweet potatoes are soft. Ideally, the satsuma juice will reduce and become a glaze.

Nano Zeringue Gros

CINCLARE'S "THE ROBICHAUX"

Serves: 1 drink

1 ½ ounces **Bayou Satsuma Rum**

¼ ounce **fresh lime juice**

1 dash **Angostura bitters**

1 dash **simple syrup**

2 ounces **ginger ale**

lime wedges, to garnish

1. Add all ingredients to a double old fashioned glass filled with ice; stir gently.

2. Garnish with a lime wedge.

Jeffrey Markel

SATSUMA ICEBOX PIE

Serves: 6 to 8

Satsuma pie may require more juice than ½ cup. You can always combine satsuma and Meyer lemon juice for a very refreshing and delicious pie!

1 (8 ounce) package cream cheese, softened

1 (14 ounce) can condensed milk

½ cup fresh satsuma or Meyer lemon juice

3 tablespoons satsuma or Meyer lemon zest

1 teaspoon vanilla extract

1 graham cracker pie crust

1. Combine cream cheese, milk, satsuma or Meyer lemon juice, zest and vanilla extract in a large bowl.

2. Mix on medium speed until smooth.

3. If using satsuma juice, taste mixture to see if you need to add more.

4. Pour into pie crust and freeze overnight.

5. Let stand at room temperature for 10 to 15 minutes before serving.

Anna Falcon Arthurs

HOLIDAY BAKING

These sweet treats are great to make with the kids, bring to a cookie swap or to give as gifts from the kitchen.

GINGERBREAD COOKIES

Serves: 36 cookies

Great recipe to make with your kids during Christmas break!

COOKIES

1 cup sugar

1 cup shortening

1 egg

2 teaspoons vinegar

1 cup Steen's Cane Syrup

4 ½ cups flour

1 ½ teaspoons baking soda

½ teaspoon salt

1 teaspoon cinnamon

1 teaspoon ginger

1 teaspoon ground cloves

ICING

2 cups confectioners sugar

4 tablespoons milk

food coloring

1. Cream sugar and shortening.
2. Add egg, vinegar and syrup.
3. Combine dry ingredients in a separate bowl. Gradually stir into creamed mixture.
4. Wrap dough in plastic wrap and chill for a minimum of 3 hours. Alternatively, dough may be made ahead and chilled overnight or frozen.
5. Preheat oven to 350 degrees.
6. When ready to make cookies, roll dough on a floured surface until it is about ½ inch thick.
7. Cut cookies in desired shape and bake on a lightly greased cookie sheet for 8 to 10 minutes. Cookies will harden when cooled.
8. To make icing, combine confectioners sugar and milk and add desired food coloring.
9. Decorate as desired.

Sally Webre, handed down by
Barbara and Tara Trosclair

GINGER CINNAMON SNAPS

Serves: 6 to 7 dozen cookies

These freeze well and thaw quickly for something special in a hurry!

¾ vegetable shortening

1 cup sugar

1 egg, well-beaten

¼ cup molasses

2 cups flour, sifted

2 tablespoons baking soda

1 tablespoon ginger

1 ½ teaspoons cinnamon

½ teaspoon salt

additional sugar, for coating

1. Preheat oven to 350 degrees.
2. Cream shortening and sugar until fluffy.
3. Beat in egg and molasses.
4. In a separate bowl, sift together dry ingredients, add slowly to creamed mixture and blend well.
5. Roll, 1 teaspoon at a time, into balls, then roll in additional sugar to coat lightly.
6. Place on ungreased cookie sheet 2 inches apart and bake 12 to 15 minutes until tops are cracked and rounded.

1982 Louisiana Legacy Cookbook

MIMI'S TEA COOKIES

Serves: 36 cookies

COOKIES

¾ cup shortening

1 cup sugar

2 eggs

1 teaspoon vanilla extract

2 ½ cups all-purpose flour

1 teaspoon baking powder

½ teaspoon salt

FROSTING

3 cups powdered sugar

3 tablespoons milk

1 teaspoon almond extract

food coloring

1. Preheat oven to 350 degrees.
2. In a mixer, cream shortening; gradually add sugar and beat until fluffy.
3. Add eggs and vanilla extract, mix well.
4. Combine dry ingredients in separate bowl.
5. Add dry ingredients to the creamed mixture, mixing well.
6. Divide dough in half, wrap in waxed paper and chill for at least 1 hour.
7. Roll half of dough to ¼ inch thickness on a lightly floured surface. Keep remaining dough chilled.
8. Cut out cookies with desired cookie cutter and place on lightly greased cookie sheets.
9. Bake for 8 to 10 minutes or until edges are lightly browned. Cool cookies on a wire rack. Repeat with remaining dough.
10. To make frosting; mix sugar, milk and almond extract. Frosting should be thin enough to spread but not runny.
11. Add food coloring and decorate as desired.

Catherine Brunet

CREAMY PEANUT BUTTER FUDGE

Serves: 24 pieces

3 cups sugar

½ cup margarine

2/3 cup evaporated milk

4 tablespoons Nestle Nesquik

1 teaspoon vanilla extract

1 ¼ cup peanut butter

1 (7 ounce) jar marshmallow cream

1. Butter a 9 x 13 inch pan.

2. In a 3 quart aluminum saucepan, combine sugar, margarine, evaporated milk and Nestle Nesquik. Bring to a boil over medium heat, stirring constantly for approximately 5 minutes, more if weather is humid.

3. Put cold tap water in a coffee cup to test candy. Drop a spoonful of mixture in coffee cup. When soft ball can be formed, mixture is done cooking.

4. Remove from heat. Add vanilla extract, peanut butter and marshmallow cream. The marshmallow cream is easier to remove from the jar with a spoon that has been in hot water.

5. Stir until everything has dissolved. Pour into buttered pan.

6. Let cool. Cut into squares

Darlene T Adams

CHRISTMAS CREAM CHEESE COOKIES

Dough should be made ahead of time!

1 cup margarine, softened

8 ounces cream cheese

1 cup sugar

½ teaspoon vanilla extract

2 ½ cups flour

½ teaspoon salt

½ to 1 cup pecans, finely chopped

red and green sugar crystals

1. Mix together margarine and cream cheese in a large mixing bowl.

2. Add sugar and vanilla extract. Beat until light and fluffy.

3. In a separate bowl, combine flour and salt and add to the creamed mixture.

4. Chop pecans in food processor and then work into the dough.

5. Divide dough into 4 equal parts and place each on a sheet of foil. Shape each into 6 inch rolls. Wrap completely in foil, folding in edges to lock. Chill overnight or freeze.

6. Preheat oven to 325 degrees.

7. Roll dough in crystals before slicing. Cut into ½ inch slices and add sugar crystals to top of cookies.

8. Place on ungreased cookie sheet.

9. Bake 15 to 18 minutes or until bottom is lightly browned when lifted. Cookies will not rise or expand.

Emma Ledet

PEANUT BUTTER BLOSSOMS

Serves: 24 cookies

1 cup butter, softened

2/3 cup creamy peanut butter

1 cup brown sugar

1 cup white sugar

2 eggs

2 teaspoons vanilla extract

3 ½ cups flour

1 teaspoon salt

2 teaspoons baking soda

½ cup sugar, for rolling

24 Hershey's kisses

1. Preheat oven to 375 degrees.

2. Mix butter, peanut butter, brown sugar, white sugar, eggs and vanilla extract and beat well.

3. In a separate bowl, add flour, salt and baking soda and blend together.

4. Pour wet mixture into dry mixture in large bowl and mix well.

5. Roll dough into balls slightly smaller than a golf ball and then roll in sugar.

6. Place on an ungreased cookie sheet. Bake for 8 minutes then remove cookies from the oven.

7. Add a Hershey's kiss to the center of each cookie, pushing kisses all the way in, and bake for another 2 to 5 minutes.

Lucille Billiot

HOLIDAY SPREAD

This holiday spread includes just about every traditional southern holiday dish you can imagine, and more. These dishes fit perfectly on any Thanksgiving or Christmas table.

MENU

PIZZA DIP,
PUMPKIN PATCH CANDIED CHEESE BALLS,
CHEDDAR PECAN CRACKERS, SPINACH DIP,
HEATH BAR APPLE DIP, STUFFED KUMQUATS

OLD FASHIONED,
CHRISTMAS CRANBERRY COCKTAIL

BAKED TURKEY AND GRAVY, ETHEL'S HAM,
BELL PEPPER RICE DRESSING,
JEANNE'S HOMEMADE ROLLS,
CORNBREAD DRESSING, HOLIDAY SWEET POTATOES,
SPINACH ON TOMATO, BOURBON CARROTS,
CAULIFLOWER CASSEROLE, MIRLITON CASSEROLE

AMARETTO BREAD PUDDING, PECAN PIE,
HEATH CRACKER BARS, CARROT CAKE

PIZZA DIP

Serves: 4 to 6

½ cup sour cream

1 (8 ounce) package cream cheese, softened

1 teaspoon Italian seasoning

½ cup pizza sauce

½ cup Mozzarella cheese, shredded

½ cup pepperoni, sliced

¼ cup green onions, sliced (optional)

1. Preheat oven to 350 degrees.

2. In small mixer bowl, beat sour cream, cream cheese and Italian seasoning on medium speed, scraping bowl often until smooth.

3. Spread evenly into 9 inch quiche or pie pan.

4. Layer with pizza sauce and top with cheese, pepperoni and green onions.

5. Bake for 20 to 30 minutes or until heated through.

6. Serve with corn chips or crispy breadsticks.

Ann Marie Chiasson Currie

PUMPKIN PATCH CANDIED CHEESE BALLS

Serves: 6 to 12

8 ounces cheese balls

¼ cup dark corn syrup

1 cup brown sugar

½ cup margarine

¼ teaspoon baking soda

Elaine Fry and Susan Stacy,
from Methodist Church Cookbook

1. Preheat oven to 250 degrees.
2. Put cheese balls in a large greased roasting/baking pan.
3. Combine dark corn syrup, brown sugar and margarine in a pot and boil for 5 minutes.
4. Add baking soda and stir, the mixture will "foam".
5. Pour the syrup over the cheese balls and stir to coat.
6. Bake for 1 hour, stirring every 10 minutes.
7. Remove from oven and dump onto waxed paper or on a clean pan.
8. Separate cheese balls and let cool.

CHEDDAR PECAN CRACKERS

Serves: 24 crackers

1 cup butter, melted

1 cup pecan pieces

¼ cup black sesame seeds

16 ounces sharp Cheddar cheese, grated

1 teaspoon cayenne pepper

1 teaspoon onion powder

1 teaspoon garlic powder

1 teaspoon salt

1 teaspoon black pepper

20 dashes Tabasco

2 cups flour

1 teaspoon baking powder

Chef Jarred Zeringue

1. Preheat oven to 350 degrees.
2. Mix ingredients in a large bowl adding flour and baking powder last.
3. Measure ½ tablespoon size balls onto baking sheet.
4. Flatten slightly and bake for 20 to 25 minutes. Cool before removing from baking sheet.
5. When completely cooled, store in an air-tight container.

SPINACH DIP

Serves: 12

½ cup butter

1 large onion, finely chopped

2 (10 ounce) boxes frozen chopped spinach, defrosted and drained

8 ounces cream cheese

8 ounces sour cream

1 cup Parmesan cheese, shredded

1 (14.5 ounce) can artichoke hearts, chopped

¼ teaspoon crushed red pepper flakes

½ teaspoon salt

½ teaspoon pepper

8 ounces Monterey Jack cheese, shredded

1. In a Dutch oven, melt butter over low medium heat and add onion, cook until golden.

2. Add the next ingredients in this order, blending well after each addition; spinach, cream cheese, sour cream, Parmesan cheese, artichoke hearts, red pepper flakes, salt and pepper.

3. When all ingredients are combined, remove from heat and pour into a microwave safe dish.

4. Top with shredded Monterey Jack cheese and microwave on high for 4 to 5 minutes. Serve hot.

Casey Guidry

HEATH BAR APPLE DIP

Serves: 10 to 12

16 ounces cream cheese, softened

¾ cup brown sugar

½ cup white sugar

1 teaspoon vanilla extract

12 ounce bag of Heath bars, crushed

apples, sliced

1. Combine cream cheese, sugars and vanilla extract until well mixed.

2. Add crushed Heath bars and mix.

3. Serve with apple slices.

Ann Marie Chiasson Currie

STUFFED KUMQUATS

Serves: 6 to 12

These are great at the bar while sipping old fashioneds! The simple syrup, now infused with kumquats, is great for mixed drinks.

2 cups sugar

2 cups water

18 to 20 ripe tart kumquats

¼ cup raisins

¼ cup dried cranberries

¼ cup coconut, shredded

¼ cup apples, finely chopped

1/3 cup pecans, chopped and toasted

1/3 cup orange marmalade

½ teaspoon cinnamon

1. Make a simple syrup by dissolving 2 cups sugar in 2 cups water. Stir frequently until all sugar is completely dissolved.

2. Cut kumquats in half length ways. Scoop out pulp with a fork or spoon.

3. Blanch the skins in simple syrup for 1 minute. Careful not to blanch much longer or the skins get too soft.

4. Remove, drain on a wire rack and cool to room temperature.

5. Combine the remaining ingredients together and fill the cooled skins with the "stuffing".

6. Chill.

7. Serve as a garnish, side dish or finger food.

Nano Zeringue Gros

OLD FASHIONED

Serves: 1 drink

2 tablespoons raw sugar simple syrup or 2 to 3 raw sugar cubes

2 cherries

½ tablespoon cherry juice

4 to 6 dashes of bitters (recommend Angostura bitters)

1 orange wedge

2 shots whiskey (recommend Whistle Pig 10 year or Four Roses Single Barrel Whiskey)

1 lemon peel

1 orange peel

1. To make simple syrup, melt sugar in water (1:1 ratio). Cool prior to use.

2. In an old fashioned glass, add raw sugar simple syrup or cubes and muddle cherries, cherry juice, bitters and orange wedge. Remove orange wedge after muddling.

3. Add whiskey and ice and stir thoroughly.

4. Express the oil of a lemon peel over the drink and drop the peel into the glass.

5. Express the oil of an orange peel over the drink, wipe rim of glass with orange peel and drop peel into glass.

6. Top off glass with lots of ice!

David Elias

CHRISTMAS CRANBERRY COCKTAIL

Serves: 4 drinks

½ teaspoon raw sugar

20 fresh cranberries, sliced in half

1 organic honey crisp apple, cubed

5 tablespoons fresh squeezed lime juice

4 ounces light spiced rum

5 ounces organic cranberry juice

7 ounces organic apple juice

4 ounces ginger beer (recommend Stoli)

1. In a cocktail shaker, muddle together raw sugar, ½ of the halved cranberries, ½ of the apple cubes and 4 tablespoons of the lime juice.

2. Muddle until sugar is dissolved and fruit is fairly mashed having released most of its juices.

3. Add ice about half way up shaker on top of muddled ingredients.

4. Pour rum, cranberry juice, apple juice and 1 tablespoon lime juice on top. Shake well.

5. Fill 4, 8 to 10 ounce, highball glasses halfway with ice.

6. Divide the remaining halved cranberries and honey crisp apples among the 4 glasses. Evenly pour mixture over the ice and fruit in each glass.

7. Top off each glass with ginger beer. Garnish with a lime.

Sonia Gaudet

BAKED TURKEY AND GRAVY

Serves: 1 pound of turkey per person

Purchase turkey weighing generally same weight as you will have guests to feed.

1 whole turkey, fully defrosted, washed, neck and giblets removed

2 to 4 tablespoons Cajun seasoning

1 to 2 tablespoon(s) garlic powder

1 tablespoon flour

1 small onion, cut into 4 pieces

4 cloves garlic, peeled

2 stalks celery

1 apple, cut into 4 pieces

¼ teaspoon chicken base/bouillon

2 cups chicken broth

¼ cup water

2 tablespoons cornstarch

Kitchen Bouquet, to taste

Chef Curtis Labat

1. Generously season the turkey with Cajun seasoning and garlic powder. Place turkey in a lightly floured oven bag, secure bag and refrigerate overnight.

2. The next day, open bag and place onion, garlic cloves, celery and apple inside turkey carcass and close bag with nylon tie.

3. Place bag in a large roasting pan that is at least 2 inches deep. Make sure the opening of the bag is facing the bottom of the roasting pan, not facing up. The bag should be contained inside the pan, not hanging over the edges.

4. Cut 3, ½ inch thick, slits in the top of the bag.

5. Preheat oven to 325 degrees. Cooking time depends on the size of the turkey. Generally, 15 minutes per 1 pound of turkey. Turkey is done when the internal temperature of the thickest part of the thigh, not touching the bone, reaches 165 degrees. Do not overcook.

6. Once done, remove from oven and allow to cool in the bag for approximately 15 minutes.

7. To make gravy, strain drippings from the bag into a saucepan.

8. Add chicken base and chicken broth to the saucepan and cook. If there are a lot of pan drippings, decrease amount of chicken broth used.

9. Combine water and cornstarch in a separate bowl and mix well.

10. Add cornstarch mixture to broth in saucepan to thicken.

11. Season to taste and add Kitchen Bouquet for color if desired. Add more chicken broth or cornstarch to gravy until desired thickness is reached.

CHEF CURTIS LABAT

HOMETOWN:

Montegut, Louisiana

EDUCATION AND EXPERIENCE:
Chef Curtis started cooking at
an early age, learning from his
grandmother Stella Ellender and
parents Elise and Allen Labat. He
has a passion for cooking and likes
trying new dishes. Chef Curtis
worked in the oil field cooking for
12 years and at Thibodaux Regional
Medical Center in the food and
nutrition department for 28 years.

*"Thibodaux is a quaint town. I like
Thibodaux because we have Nicholls
State University, many nice restaurants,
theater, nice clothing stores, Rienzi
Plantation and quite a few historical
homes. Also, we're not far from good
fishing areas and New Orleans."*

ETHEL'S HAM

When the holidays roll around, families continue to look forward to this beautiful "main event" from Ethel Block.

1 (20 to 22 pound) precooked lean ham with bone

20 whole cloves

1 cup light brown sugar

1 cup dark brown sugar

1 (9 ounce) jar mustard

1 (12 ounce) can apricot nectar

1 ½ ounces bourbon

1. Preheat oven to 250 degrees.
2. Bake ham for 6 hours, fat side up.
3. Remove the rind, score the fat and put a clove or 2 in each square.
4. Mix the sugars and mustard and pour over the ham.
5. Return to oven and bake another 1 ½ hours.
6. Carefully pour apricot nectar over ham and bake for 2 more hours, basting every 15 minutes.
7. When the ham is done, pour bourbon over it and flambé.

1982 Louisiana Legacy Cookbook

BELL PEPPER RICE DRESSING

Serves: 8 to 12

½ onion, chopped

1 to 2 bell pepper(s), chopped

1 pound ground beef

1 pound fresh sausage, removed from casing (recommend Rouses Cajun Sausage)

1 (10.5 ounce) can cream of mushroom soup

1 (10.5 ounce) can French onion soup

1 2/3 cups water

2 cups uncooked rice

Robin Landry

1. Preheat oven to 350 degrees.
2. In a saucepan, brown onion, bell peppers, ground meat and sausage. Once meat is cooked through, turn off heat and drain.
3. Add both soups, water and rice to the meat mixture, mix well.
4. Pour into 9 x 13 inch baking dish and cover with foil.
5. Bake for 70 minutes.

JEANNE'S HOMEMADE ROLLS

Serves: 15 rolls

1 cup water

4 tablespoons butter, softened and divided

1 egg

3 ¼ cups bread flour

¼ cup sugar

1 teaspoon salt

3 teaspoons bread machine yeast

butter or margarine, melted

Jeanne Peltier Chiasson

1. Measuring carefully and in this order, place water, 2 tablespoons of butter, egg, flour, sugar, salt and yeast in a bread machine.
2. Select dough/manual cycle on the bread machine. Do not use delay cycles.
3. Once dough cycle finishes, mold dough into balls with hands using remaining 2 tablespoons of butter.
4. Place dough balls 2 inches apart on a greased cookie sheet.
5. Let rise uncovered in bottom shelf of oven with a pan of hot water above it for approximately 60 minutes. Remove rolls from oven.
6. Preheat oven to 350 degrees.
7. Once rolls have risen, bake for 12 to 15 minutes or until golden brown.
8. Brush tops with melted butter or margarine.

CORNBREAD DRESSING

Serves: 16 to 20

6 pieces smoked sausage, casing removed
(recommend Savoie's)

3 onions, roughly chopped

4 stalks celery, roughly chopped

1 large green bell pepper, roughly chopped

2 pounds lean ground beef

1 (14.5 ounce) can chicken broth

2 (4 ounce) cans whole or
sliced mushrooms

1 bunch green onions, chopped

3 bay leaves

2 tablespoons parsley, chopped

garlic powder, to taste

salt and pepper, to taste

10 ounces oysters (reserve juice)

3 cups cooked rice

2 (6 ounce) boxes cornbread stuffing,
prepared according to box directions

1. Chop de-cased sausage, onions, celery and bell pepper in a food processor.

2. Sauté with ground beef in a large pot until cooked.

3. Add broth and cook down.

4. Add mushrooms, green onions, bay leaves, parsley and garlic powder, salt and pepper to taste.

5. Cook for approximately 30 minutes.

6. Add oysters and a little bit of the juice.

7. Mix rice and cornbread together.

8. Add rice and cornbread mix to the pot.

9. Stir until dressing consistency.

Benjamin Caillouet

HOLIDAY SWEET POTATOES

Serves: 10 to 12

SWEET POTATOES

3 cups sweet potatoes, cooked, peeled and mashed (approximately 3 to 4 potatoes)

1 cup raw cane sugar

½ teaspoon salt

1 teaspoon vanilla extract

2 eggs, beaten

½ cup butter, melted

TOPPING

½ cup brown sugar

½ cup raw cane sugar

1 cup pecans, chopped

1/3 cup butter, melted

1/3 cup flour

1. Preheat oven to 375 degrees.

2. Combine sweet potatoes, sugar, salt, vanilla extract, eggs and butter in a large mixing bowl.

3. Beat thoroughly with a hand mixer for 3 to 5 minutes until fluffy.

4. Pour sweet potato mixture into greased 9 x 13 inch baking dish and bake for 45 minutes.

5. While sweet potatoes are baking, make topping by combining brown sugar, raw sugar, pecans, butter and flour in a mixing bowl.

6. When sweet potato mixture is done baking, sprinkle the surface with the topping and bake for an additional 10 to 20 minutes or until slightly browned.

Stephanie Toups

SPINACH ON TOMATO

Serves: 6 to 8

Great at Christmas time because of the colors — red and green — but even better in the summertime when the tomatoes are fresh.

2 (10 ounce) packages frozen spinach

6 eggs

2 cups breadcrumbs

6 green onions, sliced

¾ cup butter or margarine, melted

½ cup Parmesan cheese

salt and pepper, to taste

2 to 3 large tomatoes

1. Preheat oven to 350 degrees.
2. On stove top, heat spinach. Drain off excess liquid.
3. Beat eggs with mixer until light and fluffy.
4. Mix spinach, breadcrumbs, green onions, butter, Parmesan cheese, salt and pepper with the beaten eggs.
5. Slice tomatoes into thirds.
6. Use ice cream scoop to mound spinach mixture on top of tomato.
7. Bake in buttered dish for 15 minutes. Do not overcook or spinach will become dry.

Jennifer Jones Rodrigue

BOURBON CARROTS

Serves: 12

6 (14 to 16 ounce) cans sliced carrots

4 tablespoons butter or margarine

4 tablespoons medium or dark brown sugar

1 cup bourbon

Sylvia H McKee

1. Strain liquid from cans of carrots into a saucepan. Add butter or margarine and brown sugar.
2. Cook on medium heat until butter or margarine is melted and brown sugar is dissolved.
3. Add carrots and bourbon.
4. Cover loosely and cook over medium heat until liquid has thickened, approximately 30 to 45 minutes.

CAULIFLOWER CASSEROLE

Serves: 12 to 15

1 large or 2 medium cauliflower head(s), chopped

1 onion, chopped

½ cup bell pepper, chopped

½ cup celery, chopped

1 stick butter, divided

salt, to taste

1 ½ teaspoons Worcestershire sauce

½ teaspoon red pepper

2 (10.5 ounce) cans cream of mushroom soup

8 ounces Velveeta cheese

breadcrumbs

Nancy Toups

1. Preheat oven to 375 degrees.
2. Boil cauliflower until just tender. Strain in colander.
3. Sauté onion, bell pepper and celery in ½ cup butter.
4. Add salt, Worcestershire sauce, red pepper, cream of mushroom soup and then Velveeta cheese. Stir until completely combined.
5. After the sauce is well-blended, put cauliflower into a 9 x 13 inch casserole dish and pour sauce on top.
6. Sprinkle with breadcrumbs, dot with remaining butter and bake for approximately 25 minutes.

MIRLITON CASSEROLE

Serves: 16 to 20

This one serves a large crowd. It can be easily halved for a smaller gathering.

12 to 15 mirlitons

1 cup butter

2 quarts Cajun vegetable trinity, chopped

1 teaspoon liquid crab boil

salt and pepper, to taste

Cajun seasoning, to taste

2 pounds shrimp, each cut into 2 to 3 small pieces

2 pounds crab meat

2 ½ cups plain breadcrumbs, divided

2 ½ cups Parmesan cheese, grated and divided

1. Preheat oven to 350 degrees.

2. To prepare mirlitons, boil in a large pot until fork tender, approximately 30 minutes, drain and let cool.

3. Once mirlitons are cooled, cut in half, peel, remove seeds and cut into ½ inch cubes. Place in colander and allow excess water to drain.

4. In a large skillet, add butter, vegetable trinity, crab boil, salt, pepper and Cajun seasoning. Be careful not to over season. Sauté a few minutes.

5. Add shrimp and cook until pink.

6. Fold in crabmeat, being careful not to break it up.

7. In a large mixing bowl, combine cooked and chopped mirliton, 2 cups of plain breadcrumbs and 2 cups of Parmesan cheese. Then combine with seafood mixture, mixing carefully.

8. Pour into a 9 x 13 x 3 inch baking pan. Sprinkle top with ½ cup plain breadcrumbs and ½ cup Parmesan cheese.

9. Bake uncovered until top is lightly browned and most of the liquid has been absorbed, approximately 45 minutes.

Carol W Blanchard

AMARETTO BREAD PUDDING

Serves: 10 to 12

1 loaf sliced bread, broken into pieces, left out to get stale

½ cup raisins (optional)

3 (12 ounce) cans evaporated milk

3 eggs

¾ cup sugar

¾ tablespoon almond extract

1 ½ cups butter, divided

3 cups powdered sugar

1/8 cup amaretto liquor

1 cup almonds, sliced

1. Preheat oven to 350 degrees.

2. Spray 8 x 11 inch pan with non-stick spray. Place broken bread pieces into pan.

3. If cooking with raisins, put them in a microwave safe bowl and cover raisins with water. Microwave on high for 5 minutes. Drain raisins and set aside.

4. In a blender, mix evaporated milk, eggs, sugar and almond extract.

5. Pour mixture over bread, stirring gently. Add and mix in raisins, if desired.

6. Slice ½ cup of butter and place pieces evenly over bread mixture.

7. Bake for 30 to 40 minutes or until golden brown.

8. To make icing, melt remaining cup of butter in microwave in a large bowl.

9. Whisk in powdered sugar a little at a time. Stir in amaretto and whisk until smooth.

10. Pour over warm bread pudding.

11. Toast almonds in oven for approximately 5 minutes and sprinkle on top of icing.

Marie Gravois and Yvette Sacco

PECAN PIE

Serves: 6 to 8

*Can make a delicious coconut pie with this recipe by substituting
shredded coconut for the pecans.*

1 cup sugar

2 heaping tablespoons flour

6 eggs

2 cups white Karo syrup

3 tablespoons butter

pinch of salt

1 teaspoon vanilla extract

2 cups pecans

2 pie crusts

1. Preheat oven to 350 degrees.
2. Mix all ingredients together.
3. Pour into 2 unbaked pie crusts. Bake for 50 to 60 minutes.
4. Stick a toothpick in the pie, and if dry, then the pie is done.

Stella Prosperie

HEATH CRACKER BARS

Serves: 30 to 40 pieces

1 (13.7 ounce) box crackers (recommend Waverly, Club, graham or saltine)

1 cup light brown sugar

1 cup butter

12 ounce bag chocolate chips

1. Preheat oven to 350 degrees.
2. Line 11 x 17 inch short sided baking pan with foil and lightly grease. Arrange crackers on pan in a single layer.
3. Melt brown sugar with butter by boiling for 3 minutes on medium heat, stirring constantly. Pour and spread over crackers.
4. Bake for 5 minutes. Watch carefully so that they do not burn.
5. Remove and sprinkle chocolate chips over top. Spread with a knife as they soften. Chill.
6. When cold, remove and break into small, odd shaped pieces. Store in closed container.

Barbara Pierson Gauthier

CARROT CAKE

Serves: 12 to 18

CAKE

4 eggs

1 ¼ cups vegetable oil

2 cups sugar

2 cups flour

2 cups carrots, grated (can use shredded carrots and put them in food processor)

1 cup walnuts, chopped

1 (20 ounce) can crushed pineapples

2 teaspoons vanilla extract

2 teaspoons baking soda

2 teaspoons baking powder

2 teaspoons ground cinnamon

½ teaspoon salt

FROSTING

1 (16 ounce) box powdered sugar

1 (8 ounce) package cream cheese

½ cup butter, melted

1. Preheat oven to 350 degrees.

2. Mix eggs, oil, sugar, flour, carrots, walnuts, pineapples, vanilla extract, baking soda, baking powder, cinnamon and salt together, place in a 9 x 13 inch pan and bake for 55 to 60 minutes.

3. You can also use 2 small pans and bake for less time.

4. To make frosting, combine powdered sugar, cream cheese and butter.

5. Beat until the mixture is smooth and creamy.

6. Frost the cooled cake.

Toney Ackman

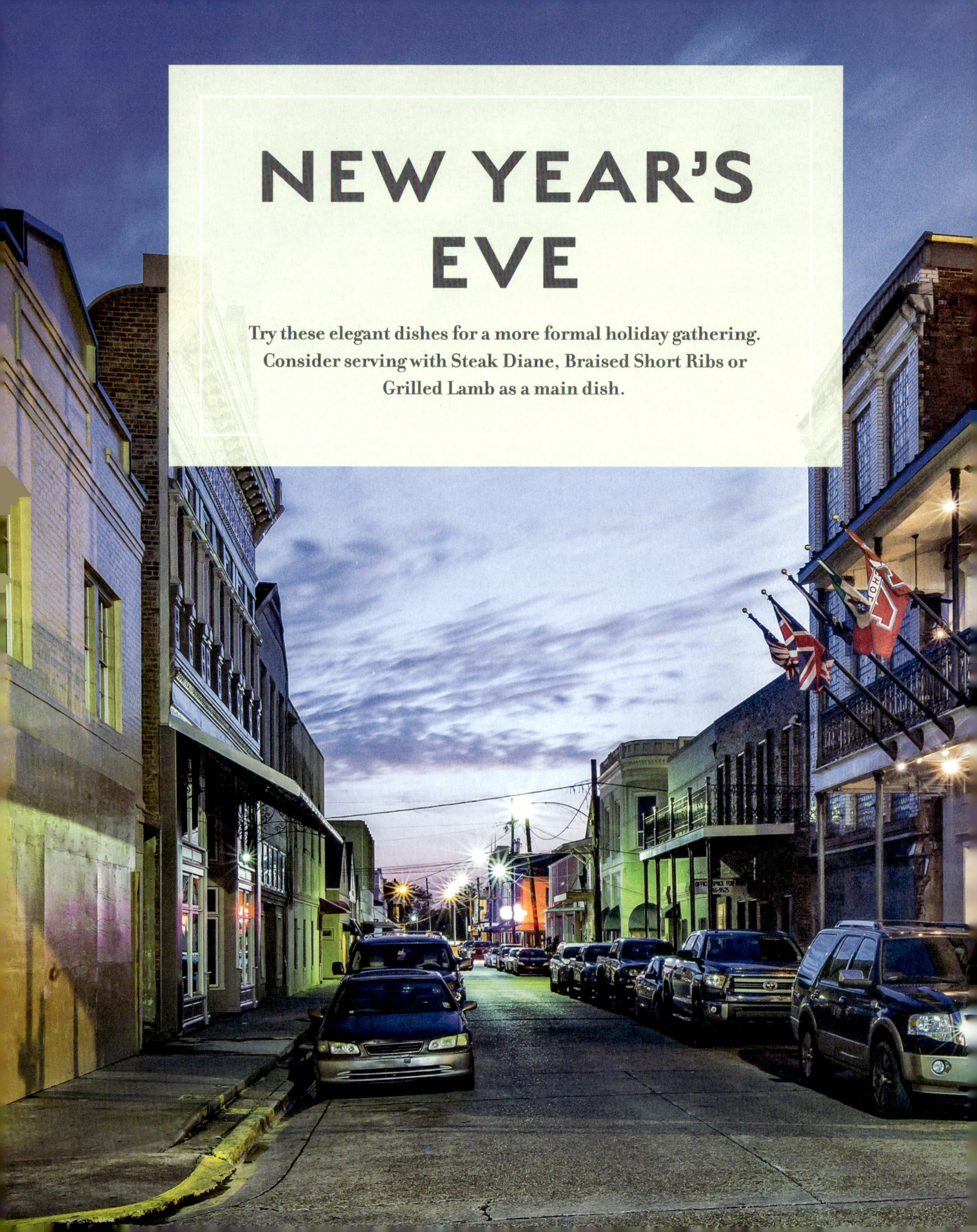

NEW YEAR'S EVE

Try these elegant dishes for a more formal holiday gathering.
Consider serving with Steak Diane, Braised Short Ribs or
Grilled Lamb as a main dish.

CRISPY FRIED OYSTERS WITH JOHNNY CAKES, CRÈME FRAICHE AND CAJUN CAVIAR

Serves: 12

For a quick and playful presentation, serve Cajun Caviar with plain Zapp's potato chips and crème fraiche. Both versions are sure to be a unique addition to any South Louisiana cocktail party.

CRÈME FRAICHE

1 cup heavy cream, room temperature

2 tablespoons buttermilk, room temperature

JOHNNY CAKES

1 cup cornmeal

1 cup all-purpose flour

2 ½ teaspoons baking powder

1 teaspoon salt

¾ cup milk

½ cup water

2 eggs

½ cup butter, melted

butter or oil, for frying

CRISPY FRIED OYSTERS AND CAVIAR

1 egg

1 tablespoon hot sauce

½ tablespoon yellow mustard

2 ounces water

1 cup Louisiana fish fry

2 tablespoons Cajun seasoning

1 dozen oysters, shucked and well-drained

2 cups peanut oil, for frying

salt and pepper, to taste

Cajun Caviar, to taste

Chef Nathan Richard

1. To make crème fraiche, in a jar with a lid, place heavy cream and buttermilk; cover securely and microwave for 12 seconds.

2. Set aside at room temperature for 24 hours or until very thick.

3. Stir thickened crème fraiche well, cover and refrigerate at least 6 hours before serving. Can cover tightly and store in refrigerator for up to 2 weeks.

4. To make Johnny Cakes, in a large bowl, mix cornmeal, flour, baking powder and salt.

5. Make a hole or well in the center and pour in milk, water, eggs and melted butter. Mix until pancake mixture is smooth.

6. Heat a lightly oiled cast iron pan over medium high heat. Scoop approximately 2 tablespoons of the batter into the pan.

7. Fry 12 cakes until brown and crisp, turn with a spatula and then brown the other side.

8. For oysters, in a bowl whisk egg, hot sauce, yellow mustard and water together.

9. In a separate bowl combine your fish fry with seasoning and mix together.

10. Dredge the oysters 1 at a time in the egg wash and then in the seasoned fish fry.

11. Shake to release any excess breading, then drop the oysters into the hot oil and cook until golden brown on all sides, approximately 1 minute.

12. Remove oysters with a slotted spoon and place on paper towels to drain. Season with a little salt and pepper.

13. Serve oysters on top of the Johnny Cakes with crème fraiche and a dab of caviar.

BERRY CHAMPAGNE PUNCH

Serves: 12

Be sure to double the recipe because it tends to go quickly. You can also make it with other frozen fruit like peaches or strawberries.

1 liter of Sprite

4 ounces frozen orange juice concentrate

1 bottle of champagne

1 small bag frozen triple berries blend

1. Chill Sprite for at least 2 hours.

2. Thaw orange juice for at least 1 hour.

3. Mix Sprite, orange juice concentrate and champagne in large punch bowl.

4. Add berries right before serving.

Pamela McCann

LOBSTER BISQUE

Serves: 6 to 8

LOBSTER STOCK

1 to 2 pound(s) whole lobster or frozen lobster tails, defrosted

2 onions, roughly chopped

2 stalks celery, roughly chopped

2 carrots, roughly chopped

6 cloves garlic, peeled

¼ cup butter

3 cups dry white wine

6 whole peppercorns

2 bay leaves

4 sprigs fresh parsley

2 sprigs fresh thyme

1 to 2 lemon(s), sliced

BISQUE

2 tablespoons butter

2 tablespoons flour

6 ounces tomato paste

3 to 4 cups lobster stock

1 cup sherry

1 pint whipping cream

1 teaspoon ground tarragon

salt and pepper, to taste

thyme, to garnish

Jeanne Glaser Higgins

1. Steam lobster in large stock pot with enough salted water to cover the top of lobster.

2. Remove lobster, peel and chop meat, reserve shells, fat and salted water.

3. In a separate Dutch oven, sauté onions, celery, carrots and garlic for 3 to 5 minutes in ¼ cup butter.

4. Stir in lobster shells and fat and sauté for an additional 3 minutes.

5. Add wine and deglaze.

6. Stir in 1 cup of the reserved salted water.

7. Add peppercorns, bay leaves, parsley, thyme and lemon slices.

8. Bring to a boil, then reduce heat, cover and simmer for 20 minutes.

9. Use a cheesecloth to strain stock, reserving liquid.

10. Use the same pot for the bisque but make sure to wipe out any debris left over from the stock.

11. Sauté lobster meat in 2 tablespoons butter for 2 to 3 minutes.

12. Add flour and mix in well.

13. Add tomato paste and stir to incorporate. If needed, add a few tablespoons of lobster stock to help dissolve tomato paste.

14. Add sherry and reduce over medium heat until half of the liquid remains.

15. Pour in the remaining lobster stock, whipping cream and tarragon.

16. Cook over low to medium heat for approximately 15 minutes, allowing flavors to blend.

17. Season with salt and pepper to taste.

18. Serve hot and garnish with fresh thyme.

GRAND MARNIER SOUFFLÉ

Serves: 6

For a gourmet dessert! Sauce can be made ahead and kept in the fridge.

GRAND MARNIER SAUCE

¼ cup butter

2/3 cup sugar, divided

3 egg yolks, room temperature

2 tablespoons cornstarch

2 cups milk

1 teaspoon vanilla extract

1/3 cup Grand Marnier liqueur

1/3 cup whipping cream

SOUFFLÉ

6 soufflé dishes, 4 inches in diameter

6 teaspoons butter, softened

sugar, to dust dishes

6 eggs, separated

½ cup sugar

¼ cup fresh orange juice

3 tablespoons Grand Marnier liqueur

2 teaspoons orange peel, finely grated

1 tablespoon fresh lemon juice

powdered sugar

Jennifer Jones Rodrigue

1. To make the sauce, combine butter and 1/3 cup sugar in a saucepan over medium heat and bring to a boil, stirring occasionally.

2. Using a mixer, beat yolks and remaining sugar in a small bowl until thickened.

3. Add cornstarch and continue beating until mixture is light and lemon colored.

4. Gradually beat in enough hot milk to warm mixture slightly and then strain into remaining milk, whisking until blended.

5. Place over medium heat and bring to a boil.

6. Remove from heat and stir in vanilla extract. Let stand until cool.

7. Refrigerate until ready to serve. Just before serving, cook over low heat, stirring in liqueur and cream.

8. Preheat oven to 450 degrees.

9. Butter individual soufflé dishes using 1 teaspoon of butter each. Dust each dish with sugar, shaking out excess.

10. Combine egg yolks, 7 tablespoons sugar, orange juice, liqueur and orange peel and whisk until blended.

11. In a separate dish, beat egg whites with 1 tablespoon sugar until soft peaks form. If using an electric mixer, beat on low.

12. Add lemon juice and blend thoroughly.

13. Fold yolk mixture into whipped egg whites.

14. Spoon into soufflé dishes. Use thumb to make rim around outer edges of soufflés.

15. Bake until puffed and brown, approximately 10 minutes.

16. Remove and sprinkle tops with powdered sugar. Serve immediately with Grand Marnier Sauce.

NEW YEAR'S DAY

Black eyed peas, to bring good luck, and cabbage, for prosperity, are traditionally eaten on New Year's Day. Try these southern influenced recipes and start the New Year off right.

BLACK EYED PEA AND CORN DIP

Serves: 6 to 8

Use leftover dressing for a weeknight salad.

½ cup balsamic vinegar

1 tablespoon spicy honey mustard

¼ cup fresh parsley, chopped

¼ teaspoon black pepper

½ teaspoon Cajun seasoning

1 ¾ cups extra virgin olive oil

½ cup white shoe peg frozen
   corn, defrosted

1 (15 ounce) can black eyed peas seasoned
   with ham or bacon, rinsed and
   drained with the ham or bacon removed
   (recommend Trappey's)

¼ cup red or Vidalia onion, chopped

1 red bell pepper, chopped

3 stalks celery, chopped

1. Blend vinegar, mustard, parsley, pepper and Cajun seasoning to make the dressing.

2. Whisk in the oil and put aside.

3. Combine corn, peas, onion, bell pepper and celery.

4. Toss vegetables with enough dressing to coat and refrigerate until ready to serve.

5. Serve with corn chips, crackers or toast.

Barbara Pierson Gauthier

BLACK EYED PEA AND CABBAGE EGG ROLLS

Serves: 15 to 20

Serve with melted pepper jelly for dipping.

olive oil

1 onion, finely chopped

1 head of cabbage, shredded

1 tablespoon soy sauce

1 (15.5 ounce) can black eyed peas, drained

salt and pepper, to taste

1 package (approximately 20) Egg
   Roll Wrappers

vegetable oil, for frying

Casey Guidry

1. Heat olive oil in a Dutch oven over medium low heat.

2. Add onion and sauté until translucent, approximately 5 minutes.

3. Add shredded cabbage, stir to mix the cabbage and onions together and cook uncovered for 30 minutes until cabbage is cooked down and most of the water is released.

4. Add soy sauce and cook for 1 minute.

5. Add black eyed peas and salt and pepper, stir to combine and cook until heated through. Remove from heat and allow to cool.

6. Working on a board, lay out 1 egg roll wrapper and place a spoon of the cabbage mixture at 1 end. Roll it up, tucking the sides in as you roll. Dampen the seam with water to seal.

7. Repeat until you've used all the cabbage and/or the egg roll wrappers.

8. Wash and dry the Dutch oven used for the cabbage. Add vegetable oil and heat to 350 degrees.

9. Fry the egg rolls in batches, a few at a time, and transfer to a paper towel lined sheet pan to drain.

10. You can keep the cooked egg rolls hot in a 200 degree oven while you fry the other batches.

11. Once all the egg rolls are fried, serve hot.

LIGHT CABBAGE CASSEROLE

Serves: 6 to 8

3 to 4 tablespoons olive oil

4 ounces Cajun vegetable trinity, chopped

1 pound lean ground beef

1 cabbage, chopped

1 cup brown rice, cooked

1 tablespoon chili powder

1 teaspoon garlic salt

1 to 2 teaspoon(s) salt

1. Preheat oven to 350 degrees.

2. Add olive oil to Dutch oven and sauté vegetable trinity.

3. When onion is translucent, add beef and brown.

4. Drain excess grease.

5. Add cabbage, rice, chili powder, garlic salt and salt. Stir to combine.

6. Transfer to 9 x 13 inch casserole dish.

7. Bake uncovered for 30 minutes.

Nancy Toups

CABBAGE ROLLS

Serves: 20 to 25 rolls

1 large cabbage

2 slices white bread

1 (5 ounce) can evaporated milk

1 pound ground pork

2 pounds ground beef

3 eggs

1 cup Italian breadcrumbs

1 ½ cups green onion, chopped

1 ½ cups onion, chopped

1 ½ cups celery, chopped

½ cup green pepper, chopped

½ cup parsley, chopped

2 cups rice, uncooked

1 (10 ounce) can Rotel tomatoes

1 (14.5 ounce) can stewed tomatoes, mashed

salt and pepper, to taste

cooking oil

2 (48 ounce) cans V8 juice

1. Place cabbage in large pot of boiling water with the core of the cabbage facing down in the pot. Boil for approximately 5 minutes.

2. Remove cabbage from pot and separate tender leaves. Return to pot and repeat if necessary.

3. Soak slices of bread in evaporated milk; set aside.

4. Mix together pork, beef, eggs, breadcrumbs, onions, celery, green pepper, parsley, rice, Rotel, stewed tomatoes, salt and pepper.

5. Add bread and milk to the mixture.

6. Make small fist-sized balls and place in the center of a cabbage leaf. Fold over leaf and roll to form a ball.

7. In a large pot, put small amount of oil and place balls in a single layer. More than 1 pot may be necessary.

8. Place on high heat until grease bubbles.

9. Pour V8 juice over rolls. Add enough water to cover rolls halfway.

10. Let come to a boil, lower heat and simmer for 1 ½ hours.

Janelle Bonvillain

APPENDIX

BROWN ROUX

Every cook can give you a special tip on what to do (or not to do) with a roux to "make" or "break" a dish. And indeed, though it seems incredible with only two simple ingredients, you CAN make a good roux or a bad one! Probably the biggest sin is rushing one. As in all forms of true South Louisiana cooking, the subject must be coaxed along, allowed to develop at its own natural pace. Rather than attempt to list or summarize the fine points, we've included them in the recipes along the way for you to use as you wish. Maybe they will be of use, perhaps not ... and you might even know a few that we didn't include.

8 tablespoons unsifted all-purpose flour

8 tablespoons vegetable oil

1. Combine flour and oil in a heavy cast iron or enameled iron skillet or Dutch oven. With a large metal spatula or wooden spoon, stir to a smooth paste.

2. Place skillet over low heat and, stirring constantly, simmer slowly until dark brown, with a nutlike aroma and taste.

3. Use as thickening agent for bisques, gumbos, soups, gravies and stews.

CAJUN VEGETABLE TRINITY

Onion, Bell pepper and Celery at 3:1:1 ratio.

STOCKS

Stocks often serve as the base of our most cherished gumbo, stew and soup recipes. As any busy cook knows, there are many substitutes for a homemade stock available in the grocery store, and often they are worth the time saved. However, in South Louisiana, the true way to make any recipe calling for a stock would be to make it from scratch. A stock is simply a broth infused with the flavors of the protein base (seafood, chicken, beef) and vegetables. A stock is made by taking the leftovers of the protein base (seafood shells, chicken bones, beef bones), covering with cold water, bringing to a boil and adding in vegetables. Most commonly we use the vegetables of the trinity (onion, bell peppers and celery) and sometimes will add in carrots, celery or garlic and various herbs and spices like parsley, thyme, bay leaves, whole peppercorn and salt and pepper. Each cook has their own version of a stock, but all include a long, slow boil, skimming off excess fat that rises to the top in the process and straining the finished product before using in a recipe. Stocks can be made ahead of time, when ingredients are fresh, and can be frozen for later use.

INDEX OF RECIPES

1982 LOUISIANA LEGACY AND LOUISIANA LEGACY TODAY COOKBOOKS COMPOSITE INDEX

LL1 – Original Printing of the Louisiana Legacy Cookbook
LL2 – Second Printing of Louisiana Legacy Cookbook (beginning 2008)
Today – Louisiana Legacy Today (published 2019)